Praise for
I Want to Connec

"Annie Chen's *I Want to Connect* brilliantly translates the science of the polyvagal theory into practical, life-changing exercises. By diving deep into the concept of autonomic states, she makes it easier to understand and improve human connection. This workbook makes a fantastic resource for therapists and their clients by making the principles of physiological safety and social engagement accessible to all."

—**STEPHEN W. PORGES, PhD,** distinguished university scientist and founding director of the Traumatic Stress Research Consortium, Kinsey Institute

"In an era where digital connections often replace genuine human interaction, *I Want to Connect* emerges as a critical guide for fostering real, meaningful relationships. Annie Chen excels at making the complex science of autonomic states accessible, offering practical steps for anyone looking to build a culture of empathy and understanding in all facets of life."

—**CHARLENE LI,** speaker, advisor, coach, and author of the *New York Times* bestseller *Open Leadership*

"Annie Chen artfully breaks down the fundamentals of your nervous system, how stress and trauma lead to emotional dysregulation, and how to heal your insecure attachment. This workbook has a wonderful balance between explaining core concepts and providing easy-to-implement activities that will make an immediate positive impact on how you view yourself and how you approach your relationships. I highly recommend this book for anyone who is looking for authentic and fruitful connections with important people in their life."

—**DR. JUDY HO,** clinical and forensic neuropsychologist, tenured professor, and author of *The New Rules of Attachment* and *Stop Self-Sabotage*

"Annie is masterful at demystifying what happens 'under the hood' of relationships. Drawing on the latest developmental and neurological research, she invites us on a journey into connection that starts with learning the embodied skills no one taught us as children. Annie lovingly and expertly shows us how our internal states affect our external relationships and how, as adults, we can fill in the gaps and missing pieces left by childhood neglect and trauma. Free of jargon, this workbook is as artful as it is scientific. With every word imbued with care and clarity, she gives us a heart-opening gift."

—**DR. ALINE LAPIERRE,** founder/director of the NeuroAffective Touch Institute

"*I Want to Connect* has a science-backed approach to deeper bonds. It cuts through the noise and provides clear steps for anyone looking to deepen their relationships and navigate stress with grace. These insights are going to help the world have more empathetic human connections."

—**Matt Larson,** founder of the Human Improvement Project

I Want to CONNECT

REWIRE YOUR NERVOUS SYSTEM FOR STRESS RESILIENCE AND SECURE ATTACHMENT

ANNIE CHEN, LMFT

I Want to Connect

Copyright © 2024 by Annie Chen

Published by

Bridge City Books, an imprint of PESI Publishing, Inc.

3839 White Ave

Eau Claire, WI 54703

Cover and interior design by Emily Dyer

ISBN 9781962305143 (print)

ISBN 9781962305150 (ePUB)

ISBN 9781962305167 (ePDF)

Bridge City Books

To those who have had to put in the hard
work to love themselves and others.
I see you.

Table of Contents

Introduction

Marina has been dreading an overdue conversation with her partner, Alex, about their different ideas of where to live next year. Marina wants to move back to the East Coast, where her family lives, and Alex wants to stay put. Because the conversation brings them face to face with a conflict and ventures into the unknown, Marina's stomach is topsy-turvy just thinking about it. She's pretty sure that Alex has been avoiding it for the same reasons. She can only anticipate the worst-case scenarios and feels tension in her body from imagining his disapproval or rejection of her desires. What if Alex doesn't understand? What if the conversation spirals into a heated argument, or even worse, an impasse that means they have to end their relationship? Her brain backs this up and reminds her of all the times he has been flippant or dismissive. In that moment, she is completely unable to think of him as empathetic and is convinced that version of him doesn't exist. She now questions the entire relationship.

Many of us can relate to Marina's experience, where the stress of a relationship challenge overshadows the joy of connecting with someone. Our brain can sometimes see relationships as complicated and treacherous, especially if we've been disappointed before. We might fear rejection or avoid intimacy. Or perhaps we too often sacrifice our own needs to avoid conflict.

Isn't it ironic? As humans, we have an innate drive to connect with others. From the earliest moments of our lives, our emotional well-being hinges on these connections. In fact, a Harvard study spanning 80 years found that having people we can count on during tough times is what makes us most happy in life. Neuroscientist Matthew Lieberman suggests that social connection is more basic to us than even food or shelter. Living a connected life is crucial for our social, mental, emotional, and even physical wellness. Bonding hormones like oxytocin help us combat stress, while isolation can increase our stress levels.

But connecting isn't always easy. Many, like Marina, struggle to connect during stressful times. We desire closeness but often don't know how to communicate, set boundaries, or find mutual satisfaction in relationships. Our childhood plays a crucial role in this. Those who didn't get a secure foundation early on find relationships compelling for the companionship but terrifying because of the potential for conflict and abandonment. It causes a constant stream of stress that makes it harder to form bonds that make us more resilient.

I've worked with hundreds of people who resonate with these challenges. They don't feel equipped to have hard conversations or maintain connection in challenging moments. And it's not just with romantic partners, either. It can be with friends, family members, mentors, or anyone significant in your life. Tension, conflict, or too much distance in these relationships can leave you feeling lonely or overwhelmed.

The good news? Our brains are adaptable. It's possible to strengthen our attachment foundation and handle relationship challenges better by rewiring the brain. This isn't just about managing stress; it's about reclaiming our ability to connect deeply with others.

Our brain can change with new experiences and learning. To improve our relationships, we need to develop more of the brain circuits that help us connect, change the ones that hinder connection, and learn to give our nervous system the support that it needs to handle the ups and downs of life.

Using insights from polyvagal theory, attachment theory, and neuroscience, I'll guide you through improving your relationships as you progress through this workbook. As a therapist, I've seen people transform—learning to trust more, understand others, and handle stress better. Improving our relationships not only enhances our connection with others but also reduces our body's stress, leading to a more fulfilling life.

Setting Intentions for Your Transformation

Getting clear on your motivation and intentions will help you make your way through this workbook, from beginning to end. Setting intentions also communicates to yourself that there is a reason to do the work and a purpose in aiming for change. Before you begin the first chapter, take a moment to imagine what outcomes you would like to see.

1. If you invest in doing this work, what changes do you hope to see in your relationships?

   _____

   _____

   _____

2. If those changes happen, how will you benefit personally?

   _____

   _____

   _____

3. How will all your relationships benefit?

   _____

   _____

   _____

4. How will your community benefit?

   _____

   _____

   _____

5. What are you willing to commit to so you can make your vision a reality (e.g., setting aside an hour a week, reading the whole book, doing all the exercises)?

   _____

   _____

   _____

How to Use This Workbook

This workbook is designed to help you gain a greater synergy between your body's ability to handle stress and your ability to find comfort and ease in your relationships. To get the most out of this process, you need to believe in your brain's ability to change itself through mindful effort. I invite you to be open to new experiences and to trust that the skills I describe in this book are learnable. The exercises, though at times simple, are meant to supercharge your awareness and lay the foundations for new neural pathways and networks in your brain. You may find it helpful to keep a journal as you work through the book. This will help you track your progress and reflect on your experiences.

Each chapter builds on the previous one, and the nine chapters are divided into three parts. The chapters in part I will help you understand the internal workings of your stress responses and what a healthy attachment foundation looks like. Part II explores how you can support your nervous system for greater stress resilience and self-awareness. The final chapters in part III hone your skills for communication, connection, and safety in relationships of all kinds. Because parts II and III are focused on developing important skills, they also feature a section called "Patience and Progress" at the end of each chapter to help guide you through the learning process.

Set a comfortable pace and take frequent breaks for rest along the way. I recommend doing the writing exercises directly in this workbook. If you prefer not to write in the book, then I suggest writing your responses in a separate notebook. If writing by hand isn't your preference, then you might use a note-taking app on your phone or other device.

Good sleep and exercise habits are especially important to prime yourself for new learning. Sleep is essential for integrating new information into memory. To give yourself the best chance to learn and develop new skills, try to get at least eight hours of sleep every night. Exercise, or any form of body movement, is also a great way to stimulate the nervous system and prepare the brain to learn.

This is a journey, not a sprint to the finish. The process is not linear—you will likely take some steps forward and then some steps back. This is all a very normal part of learning. The important thing is to keep aiming forward and to be patient with yourself. Major, enduring change to your nervous system doesn't happen overnight. Steady learning and practice are necessary, so aim for learning a bit at a time and celebrate your victories along the way, however small.

Exercise 2

Rewiring for Connection

This exercise is designed to help you experience your neuroplasticity—your brain's ability to reorganize itself by forming new neural connections in real time. Neuroplasticity is a powerful tool, and it can also be incredibly simple.

1. Put your hands in front of your chest and make two fists. Now extend both pinky fingers and point them at each other, about 12 inches apart.

2. Close your eyes and close the gap between the two fingers, trying to touch the ends together. Did they touch?

3. Now, with your eyes still closed, pull the pinkies to 12 inches apart and repeat again and again, aiming for your pinkies to touch three times in a row.

Eventually, with enough practice, you should be able to achieve three consecutive pinky touches with your eyes closed. But in the process of figuring it out, you may experience frustration, impatience, or discomfort. You may learn that getting the pinky ends to touch once does not guarantee a second or third time. This sense of unsteadiness and uncertainty as you make attempts is neuroplastic learning in action.

Building the skills in this workbook may be similarly frustrating. As you go through the exercises, you may at times feel unsteady and wonder if you are doing it right. Remember that some discomfort is part of the learning process, and allow yourself time and patience to grasp and integrate the lessons.

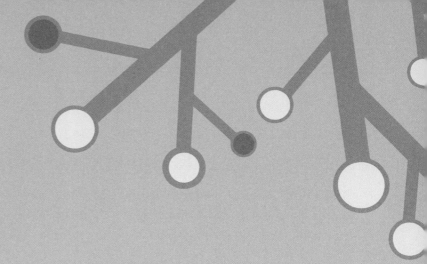

PART I

Laying the Foundations

Relationships can be tricky. Do you wonder why some relationship interactions leave you on edge while others can be a breeze? Or why childhood wounds can unexpectedly emerge when you're navigating relationships as an adult? In the next two chapters, we're diving into these questions to give you a solid foundation for understanding yourself and your connections better.

Chapter 1 is all about the stress we sometimes feel in relationships and what's happening "under the hood." I'll introduce you to ideas from polyvagal theory in simple and understandable terms. Think of it as a user manual for understanding why certain interactions get your heart racing or make you want to retreat. It's all about our sense of safety and how it affects our interactions.

In chapter 2, we're taking a trip down memory lane—back to our early years. Those early bonds (or the lack thereof) with our caregivers play a huge role in how we relate to others today. I'll go over different attachment styles and help you pinpoint which one might resonate with you.

Both chapters are packed with clear explanations and real-life examples, and free of academic jargon. By the end of part I, you'll have a better grasp on why you (and the people around you) react the way you do in relationships.

CHAPTER 1

Relationships, Stress, and Safety

Why do we feel stress even when it's harmful? Stress is our body's way of preparing for danger or challenges. The physical and emotional changes you feel when you are stressed are byproducts of your nervous system as it orchestrates physiological and chemical changes in the body. It does this to make sure that resources are in place to help you survive something dangerous or difficult. Think about when you get startled—your heart races, and your muscles get ready to either run or stand your ground. This quick response is all about survival, and it happens so fast that you might not even notice that it's happening.

However, we're not meant to be stressed constantly. When stress is chronic, it causes a load on our bodies that makes just about every illness you can think of worse. Every medical expert will echo the same advice regardless of what illness they are treating: reduce your stress. You can do this through exercise, meditation, rest and relaxation, and positive relationships.

But here's the catch: relationships can also be a *source* of stress. Some people, due to early life experiences, don't find as much refuge in relationships as others.

For some of us, the stress in relationships is as real as the joy and connection. If this resonates with you in some way, you're in the right place.

In this chapter, we'll explore how stress affects relationships and vice versa. To do this, we'll use some ideas from polyvagal theory. Introduced by Stephen Porges in 1994, polyvagal theory looks at how our stress responses play out in a range from feeling safe to feeling that our very life is in danger. The theory says that when we feel safe and relaxed, we can connect with others better and our body is less stressed. And, when we have strong, supportive relationships, our nervous system is able to handle stress more efficiently (read: better). Basically, a simple way we can measure how well we can deal with stress is to sense whether we feel support, empathy, and understanding in our relationships.

This theory shines a light on the interconnectedness between relationships, stress, and safety that I've also witnessed in my clinical practice over 15 years. When people overcome personal challenges and find their way to being able to actively cultivate safe and supportive relationships, it has profoundly positive effects on their physical and mental health. The specifics of polyvagal theory have helped researchers understand and treat many conditions, from physical ones like chronic fatigue, fibromyalgia, and irritable bowel syndrome to mental health issues like depression, anxiety, trauma, and more.

Meet Your Nervous System

Your nervous system is a vast network that facilitates communication between your brain and body and is responsible for everything from movement to emotions to complex thinking. Your nervous system helps you navigate the world and keeps you safe. To do this, it can sense how safe or dangerous a situation is (what Stephen Porges calls *neuroception*) in order to decide how your body needs to respond.

This isn't just any random guess. It's a very well-informed prediction based on what all your senses (sight, smell, touch, hearing, and taste) are picking up on, as well as stored memories and information about what the nervous system has previously flagged as dangerous. It's so much information that you can only be consciously aware of a fraction of what your nervous system is processing to make its safety determination.

If you've ever had a bad feeling in your gut that turned out to be right, it's because your nervous system picked up on information from your senses, pattern-matched it with other dangerous situations, and then sent you a warning signal that you could feel. A friend of mine once left a park during a picnic with friends because he had an eerie feeling he couldn't shake off—he found out later that a violent altercation occurred shortly afterward.

These guesses aren't always accurate, but the good news is that if a prediction is wrong, it's usually because it was too conservative, putting you in a defense state when it might not be really needed. Your nervous system is biased to protect you rather than let you down and risk harm. Let's look at the different parts of the nervous system that are responsible for your body's shift into defense.

Autonomic Governance

The nervous system is complex, and to understand it better, we can think of its role in the body as one of governance. It oversees and manages the body's responses to various situations, including stressful and dangerous ones, to ensure our safety and well-being. It does this autonomically—which just means automatically, without our conscious awareness.

Just like governments typically have separate branches that use different strategies, the nervous system has multiple autonomic systems to govern the body. You might recall learning from biology class two of them: the sympathetic nervous system (which gets the body alert and ready for action) and the parasympathetic nervous system (which helps the body relax). Each system becomes more or less activated to match what we are experiencing in our environment in the moment.

Polyvagal theory added a twist to our understanding of the nervous system, turning it into a three-system government instead of two. The sympathetic nervous system stays the same, but polyvagal theory posits that there are actually two separate parasympathetic systems: one that conserves energy and another that makes it possible for us to be calm and social.

For simplicity, let's call these parasympathetic systems the **conservation** and **prosocial systems**, and let's call the sympathetic nervous system the **alertness system**. Here's a breakdown of how they work together to govern your body:

1. **Alertness system:** If we imagine the body as a car, this system would be the gas pedal. On a typical day, it helps you stay alert and active, responding to your surroundings, getting excited, or working out. This system's approach to stress and danger is to be ready and act! It pushes your body into high gear, preparing for fight or flight. When it takes over, it allocates resources in your body to focus on immediate action and pushes aside less urgent processes like digestion.

2. **Conservation system:** Imagine this as the car's brakes. Normally, it helps you relax, ensuring you sleep and digest food well. If this system takes over too much, it can lead to feelings of depression and affect digestion and sleep. This system's response to threats is to retreat and shut things down. It takes over when we face situations that seem impossible to overcome and acts as an emergency brake. In some cases, it may even make the body faint or play dead.

3. **Prosocial system:** This is a unique system found in mammals that promotes social bonds. When active, it causes a calm heart rate, easy breathing, and a sense of safety. It also encourages social interactions by refining your facial expressions, voice, and more. For instance, when you smile at a stranger and they smile back, or when you exuberantly call your dog and it wags its tail, that's this system in action. This system becomes less active as our body senses more stress or threat, which is why your social interactions become more strained under these circumstances.

These three governing systems guide our body's internal functions. The main factor influencing which system takes over is how safe or threatened we feel in that moment. In safe environments, these systems help us find a balance between activity and rest, with a feeling of being able to connect with others. When threats appear, our body shifts into its defense modes that lean more toward the extremes and away from being friendly or social. We'll dive deeper into this in the next section, but for now, consider how these systems resonate with your experiences.

Reflection on Your Nervous System

In order to learn effectively, it can be useful to pause and reflect on what we already know and which ideas might be new or challenging. The three autonomic systems we've just discussed may be new to you. Please take a moment to reflect on the following questions:

1. When have you been aware that your **alertness system** (sympathetic nervous system) was dominant? You may have felt muscle tension, a racing heart, sweating, or feeling unusually alert. Please describe how this state feels.

   _____

   _____

   _____

2. Describe a moment when you think you may have experienced activation of your **conservation system**. This may have made you feel shut down, frozen, numb, lightheaded, or detached from your body and experience.

   _____

   _____

   _____

3. Describe a time when you may have experienced activation of your **prosocial system**. You may have felt relaxed, safe, content, optimistic, talkative, open to connection, or in tune with those around you.

   _____

   _____

   _____

Autonomic States

Your nervous system is always responding to its surroundings, which causes changes in your body's **autonomic state**. The autonomic states that we'll discuss in this book are calm/connected, vital stress, agitation, fight/flight, freeze, withdrawal, and full shutdown. What state you are in is determined by which autonomic systems are in charge at the time.

For example, when you are taking a peaceful bath at home, these three systems work together to make it so that your heart is not beating too fast, you are exhaling deeply, and there are other physiological changes that promote a calm/connected state. But if you suddenly remember that you left the stove on, the alertness system will take over, pushing your body into the fight/flight state. Fight/flight is a state where your heart pumps fast and you feel a rush of adrenaline and other stress chemicals to help you act quickly.

You can consciously be aware of some of these responses, like how fast your heart is beating or how deeply you are breathing, but other autonomic responses, like changes to your immune response, aren't going to be as noticeable to you.

Picture this: You're walking down the street with a friend, and the two of you are laughing in conversation as you enjoy each other's company. Suddenly, you hear a loud noise that startles you. Your heart races, and your breathing becomes fast and shallow. As you look around, your friend says it's just noise from a nearby construction site and everything's okay. Your nervous system should be able to relax now because there is no need to be prepared for threat. But you notice that you're still quite distracted and that your heart is still pumping faster than normal. Your friend looks at you puzzled because you don't seem fully present anymore.

In this story, your body went through three different autonomic states within a short span of time. The shifts are based on what your nervous system was guessing might be needed to keep you safe.

Let's look at the following map. It shows names and governing system levels for some of the most common autonomic states. As you study the map, see if you can guess which three autonomic states you went through in the hypothetical scenario of walking with your friend.

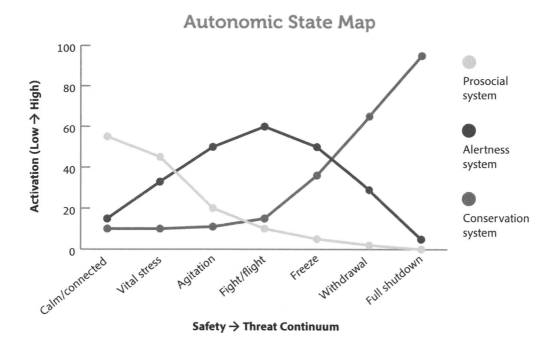

Autonomic State Map

Activation (Low → High)

Prosocial system

Alertness system

Conservation system

Safety → Threat Continuum

The green, red, and blue lines on the map show how our body's trio of systems react as the nervous system senses more danger. At "calm/connected," there is no danger detected, and the continuum progresses all the way to "full shutdown," where the perceived threat is greatest. How your specific trio of systems behave might be slightly different from mine, but generally speaking they all follow similar predictable trajectories when we feel stress or threat.

What this map tells us is that we can't pick and choose how our brains and bodies behave in the state that we are in. A lot of this is locked in based on our nervous system's sense of safety. This sense can affect how we react to and feel about everything around us. For instance, if we're in fight/flight, it's hard to think clearly. When we're relaxed and feel safe, it's easier for us to interact and connect with others. But if we start to feel more threatened, it gets harder to access our social graces. Perhaps not impossible, because we can put deliberate effort into it, but it might feel forced and fake.

Earlier I had you imagine walking with your friend and getting startled. Which autonomic states do you think you were in? You probably felt relaxed and happy while talking with your friend—you were in a calm/connected state. When you heard the loud, unfamiliar noise, your body went into fight/flight mode. Even after realizing there was no real danger, you still felt on edge, in a state of agitation. Your nervous system reacted to changes in perceived stress or threat by moving between these different autonomic states.

Autonomic State Descriptions

Here are some detailed descriptions of the autonomic states captured in the map. Remember, your responses are all on a spectrum, and this is just one way to label the range of states on that spectrum. As you read about each one, reflect on how you have experienced this state in your life, and jot down some associations you might have with it.

Spend some time getting familiar with these autonomic states, as we will continue to explore them in the rest of the book. In the following chapters, you'll see how an intimate understanding of these states in your own body can help you redirect your stress response and connect with others.

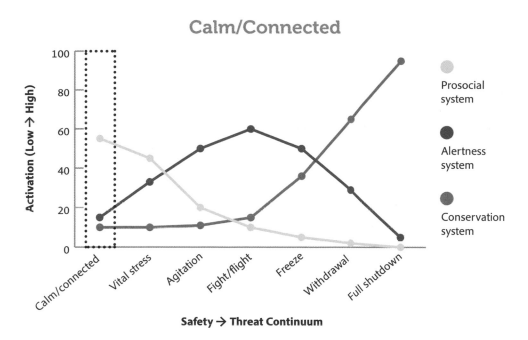

Calm/Connected

Y-axis: Activation (Low → High) — 0, 20, 40, 60, 80, 100

X-axis (Safety → Threat Continuum): Calm/connected, Vital stress, Agitation, Fight/flight, Freeze, Withdrawal, Full shutdown

Legend:
- Prosocial system
- Alertness system
- Conservation system

How it feels: You feel safe and well. Your body is relaxed. You are open and curious about the things around you. You're optimistic and keen to connect with others, whether through fun, playful interactions or serious, vulnerable conversations. You don't necessarily have to be social. You could be on your own while feeling fondness and empathy for others. This state gives you the flexibility to think creatively and logically.

Why it happens: This is your body's true "rest and digest" mode. It's the best state for learning, thinking, and solving problems. This calmness comes from a high level of the prosocial system and a normal, balanced range of the other two systems. This allows you to take on tasks that aren't stressful, sleep restfully, and digest food properly.

What associations do you have with the calm/connected state? (Examples: supportive conversation, quiet love, vibing, meditation, self-care habits)

_____

_____

_____

_____

_____

Vital Stress

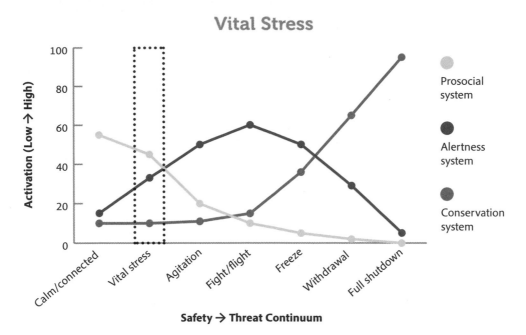

Activation (Low → High)

Safety → Threat Continuum

- Prosocial system
- Alertness system
- Conservation system

How it feels: You're alert and engaged in whatever you're doing. Even if it's challenging or demanding, you feel productive—in a flow state, even. You might be cruising through tasks or very engrossed. Even when faced with something unexpected or hard, like surprising news, you're able to handle it with a cooperative and positive attitude.

Why it happens: Your body is alert, which helps you perform or work. However, you're not in defense mode, which means different parts of your brain can work together and give you the ability to think in complex and creative ways. If you are exercising, the lack of threat means that your body can enjoy a balance of calming responses as well to counteract high alertness. As long as this alert state doesn't last too long, you can maintain a good balance and not become defensive.

What associations do you have with being in a vital stress state? (Examples: positive stress, eustress, exercise, dancing, playful banter)

_____

_____

_____

_____

_____

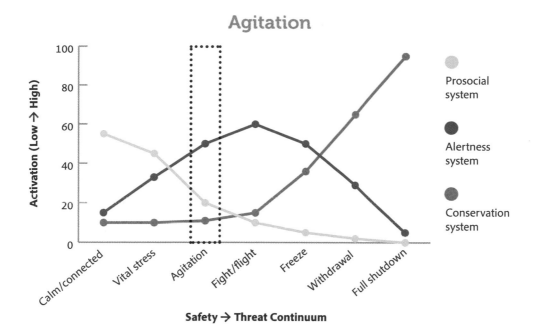

Agitation

Safety → Threat Continuum

How it feels: You're restless or uneasy. You might notice your heart beating faster, your hands getting sweaty, or your stomach feeling unsettled. At this point on the continuum, people start saying they feel anxious (they might use this word to describe the next two states as well). You could be overly concerned about things going wrong, stuck in negative thoughts, or just not feeling quite right. You may struggle to connect with others, finding yourself out of sync with them.

Why it happens: Your body has entered into the defense range. It's on alert, expecting threats. If stress hormones stay in your system, they might keep you up at night or affect your digestion and immune function.

What associations do you have with being in an agitation state? (Examples: feeling on edge, walking on eggshells, feeling some type of way, anxiety)

_____

_____

_____

_____

_____

Fight/Flight

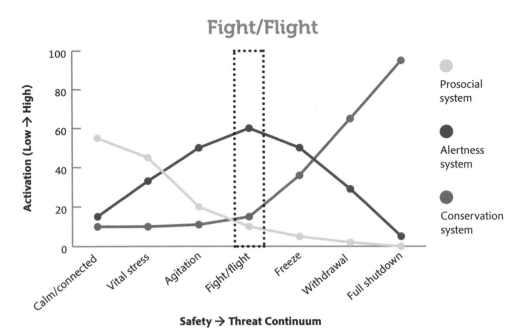

How it feels: You might feel panic, with your heart racing and an overwhelming need to act quickly or overfunction. Strong emotions, like anger or distress, can take over, making it difficult to think clearly. If there are others around, they might seem hostile or annoying, especially if there is friction or conflict. Your thoughts might race, trying to find quick solutions. Even though you feel certain about your decisions, you might not be thinking logically.

Why it happens: Your nervous system is in overdrive, flooding your body with stress chemicals to help you face a challenge or escape danger. This means faster breathing and heart rate to ensure you have enough energy. This intense response doesn't last long, since certain chemicals, like adrenaline, are temporary. Low prosocial system levels, heightened vigilance, and low reasoning skills are the reasons that you are likely to make mistakes as well as enemies in this state.

What associations do you have with being in a fight/flight state? (Examples: spinning out, being defensive, escalating in conflict, hypervigilance, slamming doors, hijacked amygdala, lizard brain, emotional outbursts, doing too much, seeing red)

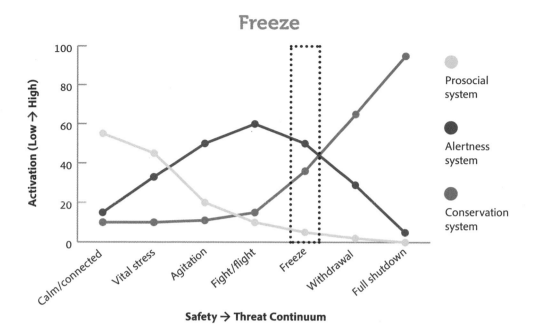

Freeze

Activation (Low → High) / Safety → Threat Continuum

X-axis: Calm/connected, Vital stress, Agitation, Fight/flight, Freeze, Withdrawal, Full shutdown

- Prosocial system
- Alertness system
- Conservation system

How it feels: You might feel stuck, as if you can't think straight or make decisions. Your body might be tense, and your breath can feel locked, like you can't get enough air even when you try to. It's like being in a car where both the gas and brake are pressed at once: the car revs its engine but has nowhere to go. Some describe feeling like a deer caught in headlights, overwhelmed and unable to act. If not completely paralyzed by this feeling, you might find yourself just going through the motions of life, putting things off. You are also more likely to start to pull away from people when you are frozen because you just don't feel safe with them anymore.

Why it happens: When a threat seems beyond escape, your body begins to conserve resources. The conservation levels start to rise while longer-acting stress chemicals like cortisol stay active. As a defense state, freezing doesn't help you run away; it just helps you exist. This freeze response can last a while, making it difficult for the body to function at its best, affecting your digestion and immune response. Too much conservation as well as cortisol levels can also contribute to problems with sleep.

What associations do you have with being in a freeze state? (Examples: deer in headlights, circling the drain, procrastinating, people-pleasing)

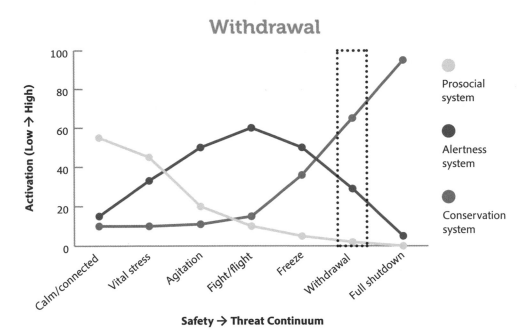

Withdrawal

Activation (Low → High)

Safety → Threat Continuum

Legend:
- Prosocial system
- Alertness system
- Conservation system

X-axis labels: Calm/connected, Vital stress, Agitation, Fight/flight, Freeze, Withdrawal, Full shutdown

Y-axis: 0, 20, 40, 60, 80, 100

How it feels: You may detach even more, not just from other people but also from yourself. Emotionally, you might feel numb and distant, and you may be disinterested in connection with others. You look for mindless distractions like doomscrolling on your phone. Some people experience dissociation, where they feel separate from their surroundings or body. If this state persists, it can resemble depression and chronic fatigue. You may have trouble getting out of bed or oversleep without feeling rested. Gut issues are common.

Why it happens: When your body feels threatened, either emotionally or physically, it switches to an "energy-saving" mode to protect itself. While you'd think this would make you sleep easily, sleep is more complex than just "switching off." Your body processes and stores new information during sleep, and being in energy-saving mode can mess with that and disrupt your sleep cycles. Robert Naviaux hypothesizes that the body can shut down on a cellular level by going into a "cell danger response," which complicates a lot of health problems. Feeling cut off from yourself and others can also make you pull back even more.

What associations do you have with being in a withdrawal state? (Examples: being in a fog, depression, blobbing, stuck in quicksand, going through the motions, sensation-seeking behaviors, isolating from others, fatigue, zombie)

_____

_____

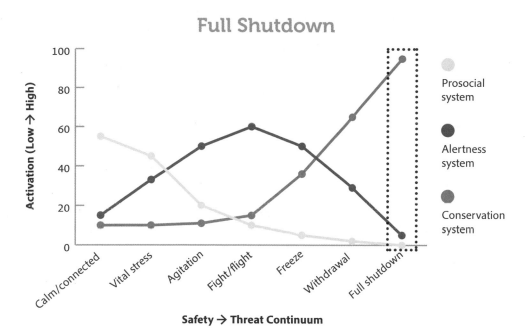

Full Shutdown

Activation (Low → High) (y-axis: 0, 20, 40, 60, 80, 100)

x-axis categories: Calm/connected, Vital stress, Agitation, Fight/flight, Freeze, Withdrawal, Full shutdown

Safety → Threat Continuum

- Prosocial system
- Alertness system
- Conservation system

How it feels: When a full shutdown happens, you lose consciousness. An extreme example is when stowaways have traveled in the wheel well of airplanes, and their bodies allowed them to survive the extreme conditions at 30,000 feet in the air by going into a hibernative state. We won't discuss this state much in this book because it's relatively uncommon and there isn't much you can do with it, but it's useful to know the full spectrum of defense responses that your nervous system may be capable of.

Why it happens: The conservation system is in full swing, activating a deep protective state. A drop in blood pressure and heart rate may reduce blood flow to the brain, which can cause fainting.

What associations do you have with being in a full shutdown state? (Examples: fainting, passing out)

_____

_____

_____

_____

_____

Are Autonomic States Feelings?

It's important to distinguish autonomic states from your direct feelings or emotions. Feelings are the conscious experiences that we might label as happiness, sadness, anger, fear, and so on. They are products of our brain and body's response to different events based on our understanding of those events and the meaning we assign to them. Autonomic states may certainly affect our emotions—for example, fight/flight can amplify any negative emotions, while a withdrawal state may numb us from our emotions—but autonomic states are not "just feelings." Think of your autonomic state as the filter through which your emotions play out. I find that I understand my own and others' emotions better when I learn to recognize which autonomic state they are being filtered through.

Autonomic State Reflection

Here is an opportunity to better understand how autonomic states have played out in your own life.

1. Recall a specific event. Think of a recent situation where you experienced a strong physiological and/or emotional response. This could be a confrontation, a surprising piece of news, or any other event that sparked a noticeable reaction in you. What was the event?

   _____

   _____

2. Identify your physiological reactions. How did your body react in that moment? Did your heart rate increase? Did your stomach feel tight? Did your palms get sweaty? Did you feel a rush of warmth or cold? Write down these sensations.

   _____

   _____

3. Label the autonomic state. Based on your physiological reactions, can you guess which autonomic state you were in? If you're not sure, feel free to make your best guess. There is often overlap between adjacent states, and it's more important that you start to tune in to your own experience.

   ☐ Calm/connected   ☐ Vital stress   ☐ Agitation
   ☐ Fight/flight   ☐ Freeze   ☐ Withdrawal

4. Identify your emotions. Now, identify the specific emotions you felt during that event. Were you scared? Angry? Sad? List one or more emotions you felt.

   _____

   _____

5. Reflect on how these emotions might have been influenced by your autonomic state. Remember, the emotion is specific to the situation and your personal interpretation, whereas the state may enhance or dull your experience of the emotion.

   _____

   _____

Calm/Connected Home Base

No single state of the nervous system is inherently superior; a healthy nervous system is adaptable and responsive to the conditions around you. In certain situations, the defense states could absolutely be lifesaving. But I call the calm/connected state the "home base" because healthy nervous systems return here as the default. In games like tag, baseball, or hide-and-seek, there is a home base where players can find rest and celebrate their wins. A balanced nervous system naturally gravitates toward the calm/connected range. This ability to return to home base is crucial, and it is what we call **regulated**.

Our bodies aren't built to endure prolonged periods in stress and defense states. Prolonged stress isn't just unpleasant—it harms both our body and mind. Even the state of vital stress, which sounds positive, still puts a stress load on the body, and it isn't healthy to do too much in this state. Even athletes who train their bodies to perform optimally know and understand that their bodies need effective rest and recovery in order to prevent injury and for training to be sustainable.

A **dysregulated** nervous system is one that doesn't bounce back to home base with ease. Instead, it remains stuck for long periods of time in stress and defensive states.

So, for example, you might have a busy day at work and be in a state of vital stress, but after a while of sustaining this, you start to worry about the deadline and enter into a more agitated state, and at the moment of realizing you'll miss the deadline, briefly feel fight/flight. So far this is a sign that your nervous system is dysregulated because of the deadline that your nervous system is experiencing as a threat. But let's say after a full day of working on it, you finally accept that the project will be late, and by the time you get home, your nervous system bounces back to calm/connected—it has found its home base again.

However, if that dysregulation were to continue even after you get home, your nervous system would stay agitated or bounce around in different defense states. Let's say your energy crashes, and you feel exhausted and like a zombie. This is an example of a dysregulated system that cycles between being "wired" and "tired" and has difficulty getting back to its calm/connected home base.

A dysregulated nervous system has consequences not just for your own wellness but also for your relationships. Dysregulation can lead to unhealthy behaviors like stonewalling, constant arguing, or apathy. When you are interacting with someone while in a defense state, you may begin to perceive more things as slights and be less able to give someone the benefit of the doubt.

The Prosocial System Upgrade

What makes the calm/connected state special is the prosocial system, according to the polyvagal model. Without the prosocial system, home base would just be "calm," with tame levels of alertness and conservation. But your reactions to stress would become more volatile. A healthy prosocial system tempers our jumpy threat reflexes. So, when you hear a loud and unexpected noise, you might get startled, but it won't be as extreme as it would be without the prosocial system, and you might be able to recover back to calm/connected much more quickly. Or, if a friend is agitated and combative with you because their internal state is driven by defense, instead of reacting combatively in turn, you might have the wherewithal to take a step back, recover, and then choose a better response.

Things will still trigger you, but when you have a healthy prosocial system to temper everything, it doesn't have to feel like life or death. You are less likely to blow things out of proportion—making you more resilient in a stressful and demanding world.

If you're curious why we would have a prosocial system, Stephen Porges hypothesizes that the prosocial system evolved 200 million years ago because it gave mammals the advantage of being able to live in groups. Think about it. living with others is far more complex and challenging than being alone. Imagine if our alertness system kept us in fight/flight or constantly vigilant of one another. That would lead to a lot of hotheaded reactivity and pervasive distrust.

The evolutionary upgrade of the prosocial system made it possible for humans to handle a steady influx of stress with cooler tempers. In order to take advantage of this feature, we simply must create the conditions for feeling safe in our surroundings and with one another.

This can be as simple as spending quality time with people we care about, where we laugh, smile, and show care for one another with friendly eye contact and warmth in our voices. When we do this, it is called **coregulation** because we help each other feel safe and return to a calm/connected home base. And when we prioritize creating safety, we also unlock the key to good health.

Regulation Reflection

1. Consider the last 24 hours. Was there a time when your autonomic state returned to a calm/connected home base? Just make your best guess.

   ☐ Yes   ☐ No

2. If yes, what did calm/connected feel like to you?

   _____

   _____

   _____

   _____

3. Which autonomic states did you experience during the last 24 hours? (Check as many as apply.)

   ☐ Calm/connected   ☐ Vital stress   ☐ Agitation
   ☐ Fight/flight   ☐ Freeze   ☐ Withdrawal

4. If you managed to get back to home base, what factors contributed? If you were not able to, why not?

   _____

   _____

   _____

   _____

What Is Trauma?

We have to talk about trauma because it is one of the obstacles that prevents our nervous system from returning fully to a calm/connected state. The term *trauma* can be daunting, but it's just the brain's natural response to overwhelming or threatening experiences. Trauma comes from a Greek word that means "wound" or "hurt," and it describes the way frightening events can shock your nervous system and cause your brain to flag things that you associated with threat in lasting ways, the purpose of which is to mount a response that prevents potential future harm in similar circumstances. Trauma defaults the nervous system away from the calm/connected home base and toward vigilance and defense.

Not all adverse events you experience become trauma. Here's a simple example: You put your hand on a hot stove. The immediate pain and sensation cause your hand to automatically pull away. Normally, after this kind of shock, your body would settle down, especially if someone's there to soothe you and make you feel safe with them. You'd learn from your mistake and move on.

But sometimes our reactions are stronger or more dysregulated. Imagine you were sure the heat was off when you touched the stove. This unexpected shock is confusing because your brain could not have predicted it, and therefore it can't figure out how to prevent this danger again. You feel more helpless and confused. Instead of calming down afterward, you stay agitated or even frozen for a while. Later, you become nervous around stoves and stop cooking on them.

This is your nervous system's way of trying to keep you safe—by flagging stoves as dangerous. Remember, because the nervous system's main job is to keep you safe and alive, it will interpret threats in an overconservative way. Once your brain stores this memory as a trauma, you can count on your body to shift into defense if there is a chance you might be near a stove. This is how stored trauma raises your stress levels and starts to limit the ways you can comfortably live your life.

It's not always the severity of the event that determines whether it becomes a trauma. Often, it's about how our bodies respond and whether we have the resilience to bounce back to a calm/connected state. Sometimes—due to stress, other trauma, whether we have support, or even our genetics—our nervous system simply doesn't have the resilience to bounce back to calm/connected very quickly and is more susceptible to processing an event as a trauma.

Coregulation

Remember how in the previous example of touching the hot stove, the mere good fortune of someone being there helped you recover and be more resilient to the stress of the injury? Being with people who feel safe to us engages our prosocial system, and therefore can also help our nervous system regulate. Coregulation is the act of making this happen. When your nervous system struggles to find its own home base, the influence of being around someone with a regulated nervous system can help tremendously.

Have you ever been in the presence of someone who, without many words, just made you feel safe and it was easy to open up to them? This is coregulation at work. It may not be obvious, but through subtle eye contact, facial expressions, and vocal tone, their nervous system was able to help yours return to home base, and in turn, your nervous system broadcasted this safety and regulation back to theirs, helping them anchor as well.

In today's nonstop, always-on world, constant agitation, fight/flight, freeze, and withdrawal can wreak havoc on our sleep, digestion, immune function, and more. Coregulation is a resource or superpower that can keep our nervous system anchored to the calm/connected state. It's about actively prioritizing interactions that nurture connection with each other. When we do this, our relationships become a powerful remedy for various ailments, offering the support and safety our bodies need.

However, it's not always smooth sailing. Sometimes, relationships themselves are incredibly stressful—such as the conversation you've been avoiding with your significant other, or your concern that talking politics around the dinner table with your family will ruin the whole evening. Perhaps you are unsure how to comfortably be yourself in a relationship. These worries can keep us up at night, signaling to our nervous system that relationships are a source of stress and threat.

In the next chapter, we will delve into attachment theory, highlighting how early experiences shape how stressful we find relationships and can make it more challenging to coregulate and create safety with others.

CHAPTER 2

The Attachment Foundation

Attachment is the emotional bond that connects us to those we feel close to and count on for support. Psychiatrist and author Jeremy Holmes compared attachment to gravity because they are both invisible forces that keep us grounded and give us a sense of security. Most of the time we might not be consciously aware of these bonds, but when the people who are important to us become too distant or unreliable, then we feel that something's not quite right.

The Attachment Foundation

According to attachment theory, the reason we experience attachment bonds is because relationships are critical for our survival. From birth through childhood, we need caregivers (usually they're our parents) to keep us safe and healthy. Beyond just being small and helpless and needing to stay alive, a huge amount of brain and nervous system development also takes place during these early years, and our early bonding experiences with caregivers shape our expectations and behavior in relationships throughout our lives. It also sets the stage for how we experience our emotions and relate to stress.

How our brain develops, and what it gauges is important or not to learn, depends on the care, connection, and attunement our caregivers give us, especially when we are in distress. This happens through a lot of eye-to-eye, face-to-face, and skin-to-skin contact. Think about how a loving parent cares for their newborn baby: The baby cries out of discomfort, and their distress upsets the parent, who responds by picking them up and soothing them, figuring out which of their needs aren't being met—perhaps the baby is hungry or due for a diaper change—and meeting those needs. The little one gets relief and smiles, which then makes the parent smile and feel calm again.

This is coregulation in action. For the infant, consistently getting this attunement and support from their parent wires their brain for a strong attachment foundation. Having the opportunity to practice coregulation from their earliest days makes it easier for them to find safety and connection in relationships throughout their lifetime.

For example, Mateo is someone with a strong attachment foundation. He had parents and grandparents who did their best to respond to his needs and give him attention when he was young. Thankfully, they had the time and resources to do this. Mateo always got the sense that his needs were important and there was always someone he could turn to for help. As an adult, Mateo knows himself well and enjoys relationships that are flexible and have little friction. When issues come up with friends and partners, he addresses them directly and confidently.

When we get less attunement and support in our infancy and childhood, it wires our brain to expect that either no one is coming or they won't be very useful. When this happens, we learn to either rely more on ourselves to cope with distress or protest to get our caregivers' attention. Orienting this way in relationships makes it more stressful and less rewarding to rely on others, and it's what happens when we don't have a strong attachment foundation.

Zoe's childhood was an example of being a latchkey kid. Both her parents worked long hours, and Zoe spent a lot of time by herself. Zoe figured out how to feed herself at school and spent most of her time after school playing video games and writing. She didn't show many emotions because there was a sense that no one cared or needed to know. As an adult, she resents her partner for not doing more in the home and being a more thoughtful partner, but she also doesn't voice her unhappiness.

A strong attachment foundation makes it so that we can continue to seek, give, and receive support in mutually enjoyable relationships, not just in infancy and childhood, but throughout life. Attachment theory believes that relying on people isn't just good for us when we are young, but we retain the need for healthy, supportive attachment figures throughout our lives. As the founder of attachment theory, John Bowlby, famously said, "All of us, from the cradle to the grave, are happiest when life is organized as a series of excursions, long or short, from the secure base provided by our attachment figure(s)."

Exercise 7

Your Attachment Foundation

Each one of us is capable of secure attachment in some way, shape, or form. Usually this means that we display the ability to trust and turn to someone in times of need. Let's explore what this might look like in your life.

1. What relationship interaction has felt most meaningful and positive in your life?

   _____

2. What do you think makes it so meaningful?

   _____

   _____

   _____

   _____

3. What do you think would have to happen for this relationship to be even more positive and comforting to you?

   _____

   _____

   _____

   _____

Holding Stress Alone

Insecure attachment, in a broad sense, is formed by experiences when you were let down by or weren't able to count on the people close to you. Let's take a moment to reflect on when this might have been the case for you.

1. What period of your life do you remember carrying the most stress and feeling alone through it?

    _____

    _____

2. What made you feel alone?

    _____

    _____

    _____

    _____

3. Who were the important people in your life at that time, and why didn't you feel you could lean on them for help and support?

    _____

    _____

    _____

    _____

Attachment Styles

Attachment styles describe even more specific ways that our attachment foundation may have formed. A good way to identify your attachment style is by understanding how you respond to a stressful situation in the context of relationships. Do you find it easy and natural to maintain connection or more difficult?

From a young age, some people develop a **secure attachment** style. If they encounter something stressful, it's natural for them to lean on others for support and relief. The attachment bond is supposed to help us feel more secure and at ease, even when stressful events can throw us off.

When people miss out on forming a strong attachment foundation, they form various types of insecure styles of attachment. They struggle more to effectively connect, especially when there is conflict. Instead, they dismiss needing support (what's known as **avoidant attachment**), pursue connection ineffectively (**anxious attachment**), or display signs of confusion or volatility in relationships (**disorganized attachment**). In the next exercise, you'll explore the attachment styles in your own life.

What's Your Attachment Style?

The original model for researching and identifying attachment styles was established by Mary Ainsworth and her "strange situation" experiment. The premise was to put babies through a variety of stress-inducing scenarios and observe how the baby sought to comfort themselves, both in their mom's presence and in her absence. The babies' different attachment behaviors were categorized into distinct styles.

The following simple attachment assessment will prompt you to think about your attachment style within a particular relationship dynamic by reflecting on a stressful scenario.

1. Think about a particular relationship you're curious to explore (whether romantic or platonic).

2. When you reflect on that relationship, think back to times when you experienced uncertainty or conflict in the relationship (for instance, during the initial dating phase with a romantic partner when you did not know how the relationship would progress, or a time when you and your business partner had to make a joint decision and did not see eye to eye).

3. What happened in this situation? How did you act? How did you feel? Check all the answers that feel relevant to your situation in the following table. Once you have finished, add up the number of checks in each row to get your total for that attachment style.

☐ I reassured myself and the other person that we could get through it. ☐ I saw the problem as a shared experience and didn't blame myself or the other person. ☐ I took time to explore how I felt about the situation and didn't rush to conclusions. ☐ I took time to ask questions and find out how the other person felt about the situation and didn't rush to conclusions. ☐ I acknowledged the commonalities and differences in our needs.	**Secure** total: _____
☐ I felt abandoned by the other person's response. ☐ I wanted the other person to do more to help me. ☐ I was critical of myself or the other person. ☐ I felt so much pressure to get it right that I acted impulsively. ☐ I felt angry and alone.	**Anxious** total: _____
☐ I avoided talking about it. ☐ I felt it shouldn't have been a big deal. ☐ I wished I didn't have to deal with the relationship in that moment. ☐ I felt so much pressure to get it right that I couldn't express myself. ☐ I engaged in distraction and escape behaviors like substances, hobbies, or focusing on work.	**Avoidant** total: _____
☐ I was really confused and felt frozen or dissociated. ☐ I abruptly left and cut ties without explanation. ☐ I can't remember anything about what happened because I blacked it out. ☐ I still feel triggered when I think about it. ☐ I started a big fight about it.	**Disorganized** total: _____

If you scored 2 or more in any particular category, continue on to read the description of that attachment style. After reading the descriptions, it's up to you decide to what extent you identify with these styles in this particular relationship dynamic. Most people will land on one style, but it is also perfectly normal to see yourself in two or more styles. Your attachment style is an evolution.

Secure Attachment

If you have a secure attachment style, you tend to feel safe in your relationships. You are comfortable with intimacy and independence, allowing you to move closer to people or apart from them without fear or stress.

When the world stresses you out, you know you have resources to face those challenges, whether that's taking care of yourself and giving yourself a lot of support or asking other people for help. You have your go-to people that you know you can count on for practical and emotional support. You would do the same for them if they needed it.

If what stresses you out is a relationship issue, you trust that you and the other person can work it out together. You might feel a little worried about discussing it, but you know it's the best course of action. So you'll find a good time to bring it up and try to be honest, listen intently, and steer the conversation toward a productive outcome. It takes work, but it's always worth it in the end.

When Elena is offered a promotion in a different city, she feels a mix of excitement and concern. The new position is a significant step up, but she deeply values her life and relationships in her current city. Elena approaches her boss, Michelle, to express her gratitude for the opportunity while also admitting her reservations about relocating. Elena expresses herself sincerely and with vulnerability. Understanding Elena's situation, Michelle suggests they find a way for Elena to take on the new role without moving. Elena's ability to communicate her needs while remaining flexible highlights her secure attachment style in the workplace.

Anxious Attachment

If you formed an anxious attachment style, someone may have described you as needy or clingy at some point. When you are stressed about something, you long for support and connection, but you are also likely to expect disappointment. What stresses you out most about relationships is not getting enough reassurance or consistent affirmation from those you care about. Even if it isn't rational, you start to panic and feel certain that you're going to be abandoned or rejected.

When you feel connected, things are great. But when you are stressed, and aren't sure you can count on someone for the kind of support you need, then you start to really take it personally. The narratives that come up tend to cast blame on yourself or others. Maybe it's that the other person doesn't like you enough to give you what you need, or they aren't competent at it. Either way, you expect to be disappointed. This might make you work harder to get their support and approval, or it might make you stew silently until you can't hold it in any longer. A lot of times, your attempts at connection come across as harsh or critical. Hearing this feedback frustrates you even more because you're just trying to feel better.

> *Ali recently joined a book club. After a few meetings, he's already started messaging his fellow club members frequently, seeking validation for his book choices and interpretations. When he proposes a book and doesn't get immediate positive feedback, he becomes anxious and sends follow-up messages, asking if people are upset with him or if they didn't like his suggestion. Sure, Ali wonders if he is doing too much. But in the moment, he feels an urgent need to find reassurance that his ideas are welcome and valued, and it doesn't occur to him that there might be better ways to do this. The other book club members feel uncomfortable with Ali and have stopped responding to his messages, which has resulted in his feeling even more anxious, because he can sense them pulling away from him.*

Avoidant Attachment

Having an avoidant attachment style means that you deal with stress by distancing. You like people and having their company—no, really, you do! But you get overwhelmed by how much relationships can demand of you. You think of yourself as a simple person with simple needs, and you wish others were the same way. The things about relationships that stress you out and feel demanding include dealing with conflict or differences, other people's emotional needs, and when people overcomplicate things.

You especially want to avoid relationships when your world becomes too stressful. That is because the things that you know will help you are things that will take your mind off stress. That's usually things you enjoy doing, like your hobbies, working out, or even working. You certainly don't want more demands placed on you in that moment, and that's what would happen if you tried to ask for help: it would take a lot of effort to bring it up and the other person probably wouldn't be able to help anyway.

> *Leo has always been a private person. His colleagues and friends describe him as a "lone wolf." In relationships, he often keeps things at a surface level. When his partner, Mia, tries to discuss future plans or deeper emotions, Leo will deflect with humor or change the subject. He rarely talks about his feelings and is uncomfortable when Mia becomes too emotional or seeks*

reassurance about their relationship. He wishes that Mia would just "chill out" and know that he loves her. This, of course, never goes over well with Mia, who says he's dismissing her.

Disorganized Attachment

If you have the third insecure style of attachment, disorganized attachment, relating may be confusing for you and others. Relationships can be practical, validating, fun, or exciting for you. But they aren't grounding or a source of safety. You can't fully trust anyone, and when relationships get more intense, you can feel trapped or powerless.

You really want to have healthy, stable relationships, but it has never been simple or easy. You keep trying at it, but bad experiences repeat themselves. It's not just them, either. Your track record makes you wonder if you sabotage your relationships as well.

When you get stressed out in the world, you might know that others could be helpful to you and at the same time be terrified of what that means. You'll go to people in your life for support, but it doesn't usually go well. And when things go poorly, you might panic or freeze up. You have strong urges to pull away or lash out to protect yourself. As a result, you've ghosted people, done or said hurtful things, or generally made a mess.

Maya had a turbulent relationship with her family growing up. In college, she becomes close friends with Nina and they start living together. They share a lot in common, but sometimes, when Nina offers to help Maya during tough times, Maya pushes her away, saying she doesn't need anyone. Other times, Maya becomes very clingy, constantly checking if Nina is mad at her or if she's going to end their friendship. The push/pull is very tough on Nina. She's thinking about not living with Maya next year, but she's worried about how Maya will react.

When Josh was growing up, his father was volatile and had unreasonable expectations of him. Now, whenever Josh's partner asks something of him, he becomes drowsy and dissociated from the interaction, sometimes even nodding off into sleep. While his partner complains that he "checks out," he says it's just being tired from work. Interestingly, this only happens to him in romantic relationships. He has never nodded off at work or with friends. His partner is baffled and feels they can't continue like this unless Josh seeks help.

Your Evolving Attachment

This exercise only asked you to reflect on one relationship dynamic. Oftentimes, we apply the same attachment style from relationship to relationship. This is because once we are used to coping with things in a certain way in relationships, we tend to use it like a template. Just like any behavioral pattern, attachment styles carry momentum. The more we practice a style, the more we reinforce it, and we can end up "specializing" in it. But if we build on experiences that reinforce a stronger attachment foundation, then we have more options for relating.

Or you may find, if you do the exercise again with a different relationship in mind, that your responses are very different. This simply means that somewhere along the way, you picked up a different template. Again, this shows the fluidity of our attachment styles, and that evolving toward a stronger attachment foundation is possible.

The evolution is not always linear. Sometimes, you may find simple ways to become more secure. But other times, as you work on yourself and your relationships, you might discover new aspects of your attachment that you had not considered before. For example, people who lean toward an avoidant style might start to sense more anxiety about their connections once they place more importance on them. Or people who practice a secure style may learn that there are certain situations that make them more frightened and disorganized in their style. Try to welcome all these insights as you learn about yourself, since self-awareness is an essential step to growth.

Your attachment style can adapt and grow because the wiring in the brain and nervous system is flexible enough to change. You are fully capable of harnessing this neuroplasticity to deepen relationship skills and build resilience. Every step, even when it is small and uncertain, is a meaningful part of your path to connection. It's never too late to bolster your attachment foundation.

The next few chapters will get you started with supporting regulation. This involves helping the nervous system find its calm/connected state and assisting it in returning to this state more efficiently, which includes addressing past traumas.

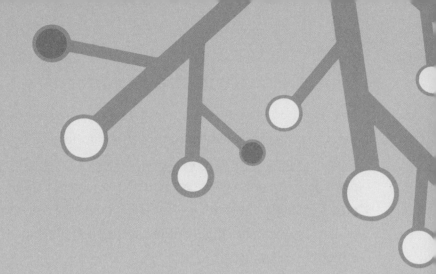

PART II

Supporting Your Nervous System

This section is all about helping your autonomic state return to its home base: the calm/connected state. Living in a technological world, many of us are stressed and stimulated to an astonishing degree. Our stress responses can get activated by the busyness of life, a lack of connection, and sometimes by the memories of our past traumas. For many of us, our health, wellness, and regulation could benefit a lot from helping our nervous system find home base more often. Each chapter in this section offers a different tool or approach to doing this.

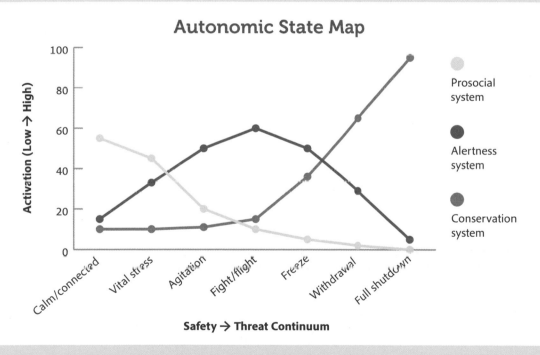

As a reminder from chapter 1, this map explains how your body's autonomic state is decided by whether your nervous system senses it is safe or whether it is flagging things that are dangerous. The three systems that drive a lot of your body's internal workings—the prosocial, alertness, and conservation systems—all have different roles, but the way they come together makes up your autonomic state.

The chapters in this section will cover:

- Becoming aware of your autonomic state
- Guiding your nervous system back to home base
- Addressing trauma
- Exploring yourself authentically

CHAPTER 3

Gaining Awareness

Tuning in to the body is a useful way to learn to read your autonomic state. This includes things like how fast your heart is beating, how you are breathing, or the amount of tension in your muscles. This kind of awareness is sometimes called *embodiment* or *interoception*, and it allows you to understand yourself better and ultimately helps you return to your calm/connected home base more easily. When you really pay attention to your body, the things you understand about yourself aren't just thoughts and ideas—they feel true in a visceral way. And the more you practice the skill of tuning in to your body, the stronger this skill becomes.

For instance, if I ask, "What makes you stressed?" you'll likely think of memories or associations. But if you also focus on how your body feels, you might notice signs like muscle tension when thinking about certain people or situations. Say, for example, you notice that every day as you get ready for work, you feel a sinking sensation in the pit of your stomach when you think about how your boss always greets you with an inappropriate comment. You may intuitively know you don't like it and feel unsafe.

You might recognize that the sinking sensation is a conservation system defense signal, and your body is trying to protect you by entering into a freeze state. Understanding this better may help you respond and advocate for yourself rather than either excusing your boss's behavior or lashing out in frustration. By tuning in to your body's internal dialogue, you'll know yourself better and have the opportunity to respond to tricky situations in a way that respects your experience.

In this chapter, we're going to explore exercises that will help you better understand your body's stress signals. The reason we want to do this is because we aren't always aware that stress is affecting us. Some people are so used their body's reactions to stress and threat that they aren't aware of the significance.

For example, in the previous chapter I told you about Josh, who would become drowsy and "check out" whenever his partner made a request of him. This wasn't because Josh wasn't getting enough sleep—it was because his nervous system was flagging these inter-actions with his partner as a threat and shutting him down to protect him. Josh came to realize that this was a stress response, and this information empowered him to make choices to address the trauma that was informing his dysregulation. When you understand your autonomic states and attend to your body's signals, you're more likely to respond to yourself and your surroundings in a helpful way.

How to Do the Exercises

The techniques in this chapter can help you become more in tune with your body's signals. While going through the exercises, focus on questions like "Am I calm/connected right now?" or "Is my body trying to tell me something else?" This might be easy for you or it might seem a bit abstract, but with practice, using techniques like orienting and mindful breathing, you'll start picking up even the subtlest hints your body sends.

With these exercises, we'll practice something called *mindfulness*. Mindfulness is practicing an intention to stay in the present moment and being aware of your thoughts, feelings, and body sensations without judging them. As you get better at reading your body's messages through these exercises, you'll find it easier to do the same in your daily life. It will become more natural for you to tune in and read your body's autonomic state.

While practicing these exercises, you might find that you feel more relaxed or that tension you didn't know you had just melts away. That's great! Enjoy that feeling if it comes.

But remember, that's not our main goal here. In the next chapter, we'll specifically focus on exercises to help release built-up stress. For now, just try to be as aware as you can about the sensations in your body (like temperature, pressure, tightness, or pain) and how they change or stay the same as you're paying attention to them.

Starting off, the key is to slow down and pay close attention. You might get bored and wonder, "What am I supposed to be paying attention to?" It's okay to feel unsure or confused at first. Just do your best and stay curious about what you can notice. Even if an exercise seems simple, look for something new that you can learn. When you slow down, remain still, and really pay attention to what's happening inside your body, you'll start noticing things you never did before. It could be your own heartbeat, a tight muscle, or tiredness around your eyes. Usually, we might ignore these signals or not find them important. But paying attention to them is the start of the journey of rewiring yourself for better patterns.

Orienting to Your Surroundings

As we experience our surroundings, we do so in a way that is either open and curious, vigilant and on guard, or somewhere in between. This behavior, called *orienting*, allows us to use our senses—whether that's sight, hearing, or smell—to connect with the world around us. As simple as it sounds, it's a feature of the nervous system that supports our survival by helping us respond to what's going on. Tuning in to the type of orienting that is happening in your senses is a great way to get clues about your autonomic state:

- **Exploratory orienting:** Imagine a calm day in a beautiful park. You're at ease, absorbing the gentle hum of nature—the chirping of birds, the scent of flowers, and the soft rustle of leaves. This state is known as *exploratory orienting*. Here, you're comfortable and open to learning from your surroundings. Your gaze seems to be broad, taking in a wide field of vision, and it wanders until it lands on something that interests you. You might notice, "Oh, there's an unusual flower!" while feeling the gentle breeze on your face. You're more open to taking in a wider range of information and indulging your curiosities. Exploratory orienting corresponds to the calm/connected state.

- **Defensive orienting:** Contrast that peaceful scenario with being in an environment when you're not having a good time—this could be sitting in meetings all day while working from home. You might notice that when you look around the room, your senses seem sharper. Your vision becomes "tunnel-like" rather than soft and open. Your brain might be more likely to zoom in on the things that are "wrong," such as your messy desk or the crack in the wall paint. These boosted senses and extra alertness are signs that the body's alarm system is on and wary of danger. This defensive form of orienting is a feature of the agitation, fight/flight, and freeze states.

Being aware of how you're orienting in a given moment can offer insights into your autonomic state. A sharp, intense focus might hint at the fact that you aren't fully in a calm/connected state. It seems simple, but it is something to tune in to that isn't your thoughts. As much as we rely on our ability to think and be clever in a lot of areas of our lives, when it comes to sorting out our body's autonomic state, thoughts can be unreliable. I've noticed that even when someone's thoughts are racing, which is a clear indicator of a system in overdrive, it is all too easy to get caught up in the content of those thoughts and believe them or try to figure out what's true or not. Tuning in to the way we experience our surroundings is a simple task that can help us avoid getting lost in our thoughts.

Furthermore, understanding our orienting state can help us guide our reactions. For instance, if you notice you're frequently in a defensive mode, you can try techniques to shift toward the more exploratory, relaxed state. We'll delve deeper into this in the upcoming chapter.

Orienting as Information

The purpose of this exercise is to help you cultivate a sense of curiosity about your current state of orientation. Are you in a state of defensive orienting (focused, vigilant, possibly tense) or exploratory orienting (relaxed, curious, broad-minded)? Tuning in to the distinction between defensive and exploratory orienting can enhance your self-awareness and help you practice embodiment.

Instructions

Right now, as you are reading this, tune in to your attitude, attention, and gaze. You may even look up from this book for a minute and notice how you are taking in both the information you are reading and other information in your environment right now. Put an X along the spectrum in a way that best describes what you notice.

Attitude:	Curious ⟵┈┈┈┈┈┈┈┈┈┈┈⟶	Judging
Attention:	Relaxed ⟵┈┈┈┈┈┈┈┈┈┈┈⟶	Vigilant
Gaze:	Soft ⟵┈┈┈┈┈┈┈┈┈┈┈┈⟶	Focused

Reflection

1. To what extent are you in a more exploratory orienting or a more defensive orienting state?

   _____

   _____

2. Why do you think your nervous system is orienting this way at this time? For example, did you already feel stressed out prior to doing this exercise? Do you particularly like or dislike this topic? Have you recently had a positive experience?

   _____

   _____

Body Scan and Awareness

Scientists can measure stress with different tools and instruments. But you have a much more accessible tool for understanding your body's stress—by plugging your awareness into the different areas of the body and noticing the muscle tension there. With any activity, our muscles are adapting and adjusting. When there's more stress or demand on us, our muscles tend to tense up. When we are in the calm/connected state, our muscles are loose and relaxed. If we are in states of defense, we might notice that our muscles feel frozen or numb. Or we might notice that there are certain muscles that always tense when we are agitated or frozen.

Our nervous system is constantly communicating with us via signals in the body, sending information about our internal state of being. For example, muscles and connective tissue may reflect tension, relaxation, or numbness, each pointing to a different state of nervous system activation. By paying attention to these signals, you can gain insight into your nervous system's state and better understand how your body responds to various stimuli and situations.

When you become aware of these cues in your body, you can intervene before stress spirals out of control. For instance, if you are studying for an exam, you might want to ideally stay in a state that supports vital stress—actively engaged but not cognitively inhibited by defense. But as you notice your jaw tensing and the "11" lines on your forehead forming, you might recognize that these are signs of agitation for you. This might mean to you that your body is getting worn out with intensive studying and you need a break. This kind of self-awareness can enable more effective coping strategies and resilience.

Once you've done the following body scan, take a moment to acknowledge your experience and try to identify your autonomic state. If you noticed tension, could that be a sign of a fight/flight response? If you felt numbness, could that be a freeze response? And if you noticed areas of relaxation, could that be your body in a calm/connected engagement state?

Remember, this exercise is not about trying to change anything or make anything happen. It's about observing and becoming more aware of your body's autonomic states and responses.

Body Scan

The purpose of this exercise is to use a body scan meditation to help you become more attuned to your muscle tension, a key facet of how stress manifests in the body. This increased awareness can guide you in recognizing and responding to the signs of stress, trauma, or overactivation in your nervous system and help you cultivate a healthier relationship with your body and mind.

Be aware that body scan exercises might bring up discomfort or distress for some individuals, particularly those with a history of trauma. If at any point during the exercise you feel uncomfortable or overwhelmed, It's okay to stop or take a break.

There are three ways you can do this exercise: (1) use the QR code or visit y.gy/guide for a guided recording; (2) read the following instructions and follow along; or (3) record yourself reading the instructions for a guided prompt in your own voice.

Instructions

1. Before we begin, ensure you are in a comfortable position. You can sit or lie down. Take a moment to settle into your position, feeling the support beneath you.

2. For this exercise, you will bring your awareness to each area of the body for 10 seconds. During that time, you will simply notice the muscle tension that is present, and invite that tension to release. Whether that release happens is not important. You will simply set the intention and notice what happens. If some tension does release, you will pay ample attention to the transition between the place of tension and the place of relaxation, tracing the transition with as much awareness and appreciation as you can. Let's begin.

3. Start by taking a few deep breaths—in through your nose and out through your mouth with an audible sigh.

4. Bring your attention to your face. Notice any sensations you might feel in your forehead, in your jaw, around your eyes, or anywhere else on your face. As you breathe out, invite any tension to melt away. If the tension eases, then notice the full transition that happens, from where it starts to where it ends. It could be a small change or a big one. In either case, notice and appreciate the nervous system's ability to shift. If nothing happens, then appreciate your nervous system's dedication to protecting you.

5. Now shift your attention to your neck and shoulders. Many of us hold tension here. Notice how these areas feel. As you breathe out, let go of any tightness or stiffness. Notice and appreciate the transition if there is a softening. If you don't feel this release, then just notice your body and know it's okay.

6. Move your awareness down your arms, all the way to your fingertips. As you exhale, let these muscles soften and relax, and observe and appreciate anything that happens.

7. Now, bring your attention to your chest and stomach. Notice any sensations of tightness or discomfort. On your next exhale, invite any tension here to relax, and to the extent that there might be a softening response, notice and appreciate it.

8. Move your attention to your entire back and see if there is tension there. On an exhale, offer the intention for that tension to release. As before, trace what happens with your full awareness, and appreciate your nervous system's intelligence to shift and respond to intention.

9. Now, focus on your hips and pelvic floor. Many people have subtle tension in the muscles of the pelvic floor. Breathing out, gently invite any discomfort or tightness to fade away. If you feel a softening, then fully notice and appreciate the change.

10. Bring your attention to your legs. Notice any tension. On your exhale, invite any tension to let go, and notice what happens.

11. Finally, put your focus on your feet. Feel anything in the soles, heels, and toes that isn't completely relaxed. As you breathe out, invite the possibility of a full release, and stay with the body's response to this invitation.

12. Now, notice your body as a whole. Feel the relaxation and ease that has spread through your body. Bring your attention to any tension in any parts of the body now. One last time, with the out-breath, gently ask these parts to soften and relax, and pay attention to the response your body gives. Take a few breaths in the current state of the body and appreciate the transition that has taken place as a result of your intention and gentle guidance.

13. Remember, you can return to this exercise any time you wish to relax and release tension. Take one more deep breath, and when you're ready, slowly bring your awareness back to your surroundings.

Reflection

1. Describe what you experienced in this exercise. Pay attention to whether you felt anything that surprised you, was unfamiliar, or was either uncomfortable or pleasurable.

   _____

   _____

   _____

   _____

2. What was it like to focus on and appreciate the nervous system's response to your invitation to soften?

   _____

   _____

   _____

   _____

   _____

Diaphragmatic Breathing

Your breathing is another important window into your body's autonomic state, and being able to identify the specifics of your breathing can help you understand stress and dysregulation better.

Diaphragmatic breathing describes breathing deeply and steadily with your diaphragm (a muscle in your belly area), which happens naturally when you are relaxed. Breathing in this way helps you draw in air with less effort. Because it is more efficient for your body than other types of breathing, it is ideal for your body's natural relaxation and recharge processes and corresponds to the calm/connected state.

Let's visualize the diaphragm and how it helps us breathe. The diaphragm is a large, thin, dome-shaped layer of muscle that separates the lungs and belly organs. It looks kind of like the dome of a tent, with the lungs resting on top of the tent and the belly organs inside the tent. To draw air in, this domed muscle contracts and flattens down toward your pelvis in order to make space in the lung cavity for the lungs to expand with air. When this happens, the organs below the diaphragm get a bit of a "massage," and your belly expands. When you exhale, the diaphragm relaxes and returns to its dome position.

When you use your diaphragm to breathe, it's the contractions of this muscle that expand the lungs and draw in air. The release of air from your lungs then allows the diaphragm to relax again.

Want a closer look? Here's a video that shows the mechanics of the lungs, heart, and diaphragm inside the body of a person breathing: y.gy/guide. Please take a moment to study the model and visualize the diaphragm in your own body. Studying and internalizing the mechanics will help you learn diaphragmatic breathing.

Chest breathing, on the other hand, is associated with alertness stress states. It relies more on the muscles in the neck, shoulders, and chest to expand the chest and draw air in and out of the lungs. It is a powerful way to get air in and out of the lungs quickly (almost like gasping), but it's not as efficient for the body as diaphragmatic breathing. It's good to chest breathe for short periods of time when we need more oxygen, like when we exercise.

But when we live in extended periods of stress and perceived threat, our body can "forget" how to breathe properly using the diaphragm, and we instead default to chest breathing all or most of the time. This reinforces stress and anxiety. Teaching our body to breathe using the diaphragm again can help us access the calm/connected state more easily.

The breath can also slow so much that you begin to feel slightly lightheaded or sluggish. This could be characteristic of a breathing pattern that is associated with the activation of the conservation system, which takes over in the freeze state and is in full swing with the withdrawal state. With your nervous system in a freeze response, you might experience "air hunger" or find it difficult to take in full breaths. This kind of breathing pattern gets your body less oxygen, which is what contributes to you feeling shut down, numb, or sleepy.

Here is a guide to common breath patterns and their associated nervous system response:

Autonomic State	Characteristics
Calm/connected	• Breathing is connected to the movement of the diaphragm, with little to no help from the neck and chest muscles.
Vital stress	• Breaths can vary between fuller and more shallow, but breathing generally flows easily.
Agitation	• There may be a shift from belly breathing to chest breathing with help from the accessory muscles in the neck and chest.
Fight or flight	• Breathing is shallow and rapid, with noticeable speeding up of the heart rate. • Chest breathing is common.
Freeze	• Air may feel restricted, constricted, or even held. • Breaths may be shallow and barely noticeable, even with effort.
Withdrawal	• Breathing is slowed and subdued, with a dazed quality. • Irregular pauses or erratic breathing are possible as the body switches between shutting down and activation.

If you practice diaphragmatic breathing every day over the course of several weeks or months, you can reteach your nervous system to primarily use the diaphragm to breathe again. This supports regulation in a tangible way by making it easier for your nervous system to remember and find its home base again. I also find that diaphragmatic breathing helps us become more conscious of the body's signals—recognizing more easily when it is in a calm/connected state and when it is not.

Myths of Belly Breathing

Let's address some common misconceptions about belly breathing:

Myth	Reality
Belly breathing is taking deep breaths or filling the lungs with as much air as possible.	When you draw in air by engaging the diaphragm, you can draw in as much or as little air as you like. Conversely, you can also take deep breaths by using the chest and neck muscles. Belly breathing is not about air volume, but about what muscles initiate the inhale.
Your chest should remain still, and only your belly should move.	Your upper chest should move less, but it will still move. Breathing is always a very dynamic activity involving moving parts that are all connected. When the diaphragm contracts and flattens to draw air in, it expands the lungs, which requires some movement throughout the chest as well.
You develop really strong abdominal/core muscles when you belly breathe.	Your diaphragm is doing the work here, not your abdominal muscles. Even as you "work out" your diaphragm via belly breathing, your core should only be keeping your torso balanced over your pelvis if you are upright. If you are lying down, your abdominal muscles should be relaxed.

Diaphragmatic Breathing

In this exercise, you will practice breathing with your diaphragm for five minutes while lying down. I recommend doing this exercise at least once a day. It only takes five minutes, but it will build the foundation for you to be able to consciously recognize how the breath behaves in the calm/connected state and help your nervous system strengthen its connection with the diaphragm in breathing.

Instructions

1. Choose a quiet and comfortable space where you can lie down on your back.

2. Set a timer for five minutes.

3. As you visualize your diaphragm contracting downward, slowly breathe in through your nose. You should see more expansion in the belly than in the upper chest as you breathe in. You may not be able to feel the diaphragm itself, but see if you can feel a gentle massage in your belly organs as you inhale.

4. Slowly breathe out, imagining the diaphragm returning to its dome position.

5. Notice if any other parts of your body are tense and invite these parts to relax.

6. Continue breathing with your diaphragm until the timer goes off.

7. At the end of five minutes, either stand or sit up, and see if you can take three more diaphragmatic breaths in an upright position.

8. After a week or two of doing the exercise daily while lying down, feel free to do it while sitting or standing up. Lying down is easier and will help you build a better sense of your body's breathing mechanics, so that is why you want to start there.

Some people have trouble engaging the diaphragm or getting other muscles to relax the first time they try. It's okay if you can only take in a small breath with the diaphragm or even if you need to stop and study the interactive video until you feel ready to try again. At first, belly breathing may feel unfamiliar to you. But if you practice it often during the day in different positions (lying down, sitting, and standing), then over time you will have a stronger diaphragm, and breathing in this way will be more comfortable and automatic.

Diaphragmatic breathing isn't a quick fix for anxiety or stress. While it can provide immediate relief in some situations, it is most effective when practiced regularly and combined with other stress management techniques, such as mindfulness, meditation, and physical exercise.

Troubleshooting and Further Advice

If you notice your autonomic state shift toward more threat states when you focus on your breathing in this exercise, you can do several things:

- Take a pause and try again.

- If doing it while lying down was fine but you get activated when doing it upright, then just do it lying down.

- Instead of doing the exercise, study the diaphragmatic breathing video and visualize your own body doing it.

- If you continue to experience more activation, you can gently back off and say to yourself, "Thank you, nervous system, for staying vigilant to keep me alive."

Exercise 13

Autonomic State Log

After practicing orienting, body scanning, and diaphragmatic breathing to establish some conscious awareness of your body, you are now ready to do a full day's log of recording your autonomic state.

It's natural for your autonomic state—your body's response to stress and threat—to fluctuate throughout the day as your nervous system responds to what the environment demands. Remember, there is no right or wrong state to be in. But ideally, you return to "home base" and stay in the calm/connected state as often as possible.

Instructions

Pick a day when you will pay attention to your autonomic state throughout the day. Use what you have learned to monitor your muscle tension, breathing, and orienting as often as possible. You can either record your results in real time throughout the day as you notice changes or schedule notifications for yourself every two hours and record your results then. For each two-hour increment in the following chart, check as many states as you were able to detect in your body. If you could use a refresher on the different states, refer back to the descriptions in chapter 1.

For each two-hour period where you checked the calm/connected box, we can consider your nervous system regulated for that period of time. However, for the two-hour periods where you did not check that box, your nervous system was dysregulated. Your goal will be to spend some time in the calm/connected state for almost all of the two-hour periods in your day. In the next chapter, we will explore some strategies that can help your nervous system regulate.

Day:	Calm/ Connected	Vital Stress	Agitation	Fight/Flight	Freeze	Withdrawal
6 a.m.–8 a.m.						
8 a.m.–10 a.m.						
10 a.m.–12 p.m.						
12 p.m.–2 p.m.						
2 p.m.–4 p.m.						
4 p.m.–6 p.m.						
6 p.m.–8 p.m.						
8 p.m.–10 p.m.						
10 p.m.–12 a.m.						
Total (Add checks in each column)						

Patience and Progress

Learning to tune in to the nervous system is a process that takes practice, patience, and curiosity. The exercises I've offered in this chapter are foundational in the journey to find regulation in your nervous system, and I encourage you to do them regularly for two to four weeks to see results:

- Orienting: throughout the day everyday

- Body scan: two to three times per week

- Diaphragmatic breathing: twice a day for five minutes

These are simple, free practices. But in order to use them in your life regularly, you might have to overcome some natural tendency we all have to stick with what we already know. Your brain will probably resist and try to dismiss the importance of these practices or procrastinate. This is because forming new somatic connections is one of the hardest things for your brain to learn. But if you put in the time and focus, you will be greatly rewarded with the ability to take charge of your health, stress, and relationships.

At first you might not even be sure you are doing it right. Catching yourself in a moment when you can actually slow down and detect your breathing or orienting might seem accidental. But the more you do it, the better you will get at it. When you manage to practice, give yourself a pat on the back for building a new skill.

Eventually you will be able to do it more reliably and the information you deduce about your autonomic state will become more useful and interesting, leading to further curiosity—"I wonder how often I orient like this during the day" or "I wonder how I typically breathe when I am with my family." Being able to engage and stay curious at each step is the kind of progress you want to aim for.

The awareness you are growing for your autonomic state will be handy in the next chapter, where you'll explore techniques to guide your nervous system back to calm/connected.

CHAPTER 4

Finding Your Calm/ Connected Home Base

In the previous chapter, you learned to identify your autonomic state and notice signs of dysregulation. Now let's explore exercises to guide your nervous system from stress and threat states back to calm/connected. This is what I call "returning to home base." Finding your own home base—in other words, being able to center yourself in a calm/connected state—is a skill of utmost importance.

Learning to create these shifts in real time will help you face challenges and stressful situations. You can be more confident in life and in relationships—even when something stresses you out—because you know that you can listen to your body's signals and help your nervous system orient toward safety again. Being able to steady yourself back to a calm/connected state provides a platform for self-knowing and makes it easier to learn and practice effective communication and coregulation skills. It will ultimately help you grow a stronger attachment foundation because it will give you more resilience and endurance to get through the ups and downs of relationships.

Shifting from other states back to calm/connected doesn't have to be hard. Your nervous system is a marvel, continually adapting and responding. Everything from your thoughts and actions to a slight breeze on your skin can influence your nervous system's response. The real magic isn't in how special a technique is but in understanding and harnessing your nervous system's adaptability. Not every technique will resonate with you, but with intention, you can discover what is effective.

For example, breathing exercises can be an amazing tool for shifting autonomic state. But for some people who have experienced trauma, focusing on the breath can trigger dysregulation. So, rather than take for granted that a technique will work as intended, what's more important is that you develop the ability to read what actually happens inside your body, whether it is a shift toward calm/connected, movement into a different autonomic state, or no change at all.

This chapter is all about putting techniques to the test within your own nervous system and learning what works for you. The skills you built in the previous chapter will help you here in detecting and reading your body's signals.

The following are all signs your body is shifting to calm/connected:

- You experience a spontaneous yawn or sigh

- Tense muscles relax (especially in the forehead, eyes, jaw, neck, shoulders, belly, and pelvic floor)

- Your breath syncs more with your heartbeat

- You begin breathing with your diaphragm

- You feel more present

- You feel love or empathy toward yourself or others

- You feel safer and more open

The most important thing is that you learn to use whatever tools you have at your disposal to shift back to calm/connected and you are able to recognize the subtleties of this shift with practice.

Communicating with Your Body

Have you ever tried to talk yourself out of feeling anxious? Did this immediately shift your autonomic state? If so, then that is very fortunate. Many people continue to feel anxious—or even feel worse because they become convinced that everything is fine and that their body is doing something it's not supposed to. The nervous system doesn't usually override its own survival instincts because you consciously tell it to.

Your nervous system operates around the clock to ensure your survival. It's constantly taking in information from every possible source and adjusting your body's responses. It does all this without needing any conscious input. This is for good reason. Compared to the steady and unwavering functioning of the autonomic nervous system, the conscious mind is unreliable and slow. If our survival depended on our fickle and easily distracted conscious thoughts, we wouldn't survive a day. In simple terms, the business of keeping us alive is the job of the autonomic nervous system, not your conscious thoughts.

But here's the key: To effectively shift your nervous system toward a calm/connected state, you can provide it with different data. By making deliberate changes in your body, like adjusting your breath, muscle tension, and sensory orientation, you give your nervous system new, meaningful information. The simple act of cuing the breath allows the nervous system to recognize information about the body being safe and perhaps adapt with it. By employing such techniques, you're not overriding the autonomic nervous system; you're engaging in a call-and-response dialogue with it.

It's like this: You'll notice your body's tension and defense signals. Then, you'll communicate with your nervous system by initiating a calming breath, for example. Doing this is kind of like asking the nervous system, "Can you take this cue and relax everything else?" And its response could be "yes," in which case, you'll feel a ripple of relaxation throughout other parts of your body. If this happens, try to fully appreciate the body's transition from defense and toward calm/connected, and enjoy it.

Or the nervous system might respond "no" and remain on alert because it is still flagging and processing danger. In this case, you'll feel your body meet you with resistance, such as ongoing muscle tension or your breathing quickly reverting back to chest breathing. If this happens, it's okay. Right now, it's more important to practice the dialogue and notice the response, even if that's a small shift toward calm/connected or none at all. Try to embrace all versions of what can happen.

As you practice, you'll refine your skills, gradually finding it easier to transition to a calm/connected state. You will get better at working *with* the nervous system to create this shift. For now, just enjoy the exercises in this chapter, engage in them with deliberate curiosity, and start to build your self-awareness and attunement. Each exercise includes notes and recommendations about when to use it. But in general, finding ways to intentionally shift toward calm/connected is something you can and should do as often as possible. In our ever-stressful modern world, pausing to reconnect with calmness is more than a luxury—it's a necessity.

Exploratory Orienting

In this exercise, you will practice shifting into exploratory orienting and anchoring there in order to help your nervous system find its way back to your home base of calm/connected. When you engage in exploratory orienting, you become present in the moment and focus on appreciating the environment around you. Remember, if you notice discomfort during the exercise, take it as a sign to go slower or take a pause.

Shifting into exploratory orienting can be particularly helpful when you are in an agitation or freeze response. You can also do it during short breaks when you are working for long periods of time. It can help prevent your nervous system from getting stuck in stress mode.

Pre-Assessment

Which autonomic state best describes what you feel right now?

- ☐ Calm/connected
- ☐ Vital stress
- ☐ Agitation
- ☐ Fight/flight
- ☐ Freeze
- ☐ Withdrawal

Instructions

1. Choose a quiet and comfortable space, either indoors or outdoors.

2. Sit comfortably and close your eyes for a few moments until you feel more still.

3. Open your eyes and let your gaze go wherever it wants to go, turning your head as needed.

4. When it feels right, let your eyes rest on an object for a while. See this object with curiosity, as if you're seeing it for the first time. Try to engage all your senses. What can you smell? What can you hear? Can you feel the temperature or any breeze on your skin?

5. When you feel ready, gently move your gaze to another object and repeat.

6. Continue for one to five minutes, allowing your eyes to rest on the different objects in your environment, surrounding you on all sides.

Post-Assessment

Which autonomic state best describes what you feel right now?

☐ Calm/connected   ☐ Vital stress   ☐ Agitation

☐ Fight/flight   ☐ Freeze   ☐ Withdrawal

Describe any changes you noticed in your body, emotions, or thoughts either during or after the exercise.

_____

_____

_____

_____

Progressive Muscle Relaxation

Our muscles are quick to activate with stress and sometimes slow to return to home base. As a result, we often continue to carry muscle tension throughout the day, far after the stress response has outlived its usefulness. This exercise involves tensing and relaxing muscles in your body in a sequence. There are three ways you can do this exercise: (1) use the QR code or visit y.gy/guide for a guided recording; (2) read the following instructions and follow along; or (3) record yourself reading the instructions for a guided prompt in your own voice.

This exercise is particularly recommended if you need to relax yourself to fall asleep or whenever you can make time during the day to get into a deeper relaxed state.

Pre-Assessment
Which autonomic state best describes what you feel right now?

☐ Calm/connected   ☐ Vital stress   ☐ Agitation
☐ Fight/flight   ☐ Freeze   ☐ Withdrawal

Instructions
1. Choose a quiet, comfortable space where you can either sit upright in a chair with your feet flat on the ground or lie down on a flat surface, such as a floor, yoga mat, or bed.

2. Close your eyes and take a few deep breaths to help you relax and focus your attention on your body. We'll start at the feet and work up to the head. At each step, you'll tense and hold only the muscles in the area of focus for a count of 5, and then release completely for a count of 10. Aim for about 50 to 70 percent tension of the muscle each time.

3. Now we'll begin.
   a. **Feet:** Curl your toes, feeling the tension in the arches of your feet. Now, slowly release the tension and relax.

   b. **Calves:** Tighten your calf muscles by pointing your toes upward, toward your knees. Slowly release the tension and relax.

   c. **Thighs:** Tense your thigh muscles. You can press your knees together if it's easier. Slowly release the tension and relax.

d. **Pelvic floor:** Squeeze your pelvic floor and seat muscles. Slowly release the tension and relax.

e. **Abdomen:** Tighten your abdominal muscles. Slowly release the tension and relax.

f. **Upper back and shoulders:** Shrug your shoulders up toward your ears, feeling the tension in your upper back and shoulder muscles. Slowly release the tension and relax.

g. **Arms:** Tense your upper arm and forearm muscles by imagining stiffening your elbow joint. Slowly release the tension and relax.

h. **Hands:** Make tight fists, feeling the tension in your hands and forearms. Slowly release the tension and relax.

i. **Neck:** Tilt your head forward to tense your neck, feeling the tension on all sides of the neck. Slowly release the tension and relax.

j. **Face:** Scrunch up your facial muscles, including your eyes, nose, and mouth. Slowly release the tension and relax.

4. Take a few deep breaths, focusing on the sensation of relaxation throughout your body.

5. Allow yourself to rest for a moment, enjoying the feeling of relaxation in your muscles.

6. Slowly open your eyes and bring your awareness back to your surroundings.

If you practice this exercise regularly, you'll improve your mind-body connection and notice when your muscles are unnecessarily tense throughout the day. It will help your nervous system anchor more in a calm/connected state.

Post-Assessment

Which autonomic state best describes what you feel right now?

☐ Calm/connected   ☐ Vital stress   ☐ Agitation
☐ Fight/flight   ☐ Freeze   ☐ Withdrawal

Describe any changes you noticed in your body, emotions, or thoughts either during or after the exercise.

_____

_____

_____

_____

Physiological Sigh

This exercise will guide you through the "physiological sigh," a calming breathing technique popularized by neuroscientist Andrew Huberman that reduces stress. The physiological sigh involves taking two short, consecutive inhales followed by a longer, slow exhale. This pattern of breathing can help to lower heart rate, reduce anxiety, and promote relaxation.

Huberman recommends doing this exercise when you feel stressed or anxious. I find this technique particularly helpful when in a state of freeze or withdrawal.

Pre-Assessment

Which autonomic state best describes what you feel right now?

☐ Calm/connected   ☐ Vital stress   ☐ Agitation
☐ Fight/flight   ☐ Freeze   ☐ Withdrawal

Instructions

1. Find a comfortable position.

2. Inhale twice quickly: Inhale once through your nose, filling your lungs most of the way. Then inhale again, filling your lungs completely.

3. Slowly exhale, releasing the air in a controlled manner.

4. Repeat for three to five cycles or as long as it feels comfortable for you.

5. Pause for a moment, allowing your breath to return to its natural rhythm. Notice any changes in your heart rate, muscle tension, or overall sense of relaxation.

Post-Assessment

Which autonomic state best describes what you feel right now?

☐ Calm/connected   ☐ Vital stress   ☐ Agitation
☐ Fight/flight   ☐ Freeze   ☐ Withdrawal

Describe any changes you noticed in your body, emotions, or thoughts either during or after the exercise.

_____

_____

_____

_____

Hot-Air Balloon Exhale

This simple breathing technique is designed to help you return to a calm/connected state by practicing an incremental extended exhale. Imagine a hot-air balloon in the sky. In order to land, the operator vents air out in increments, or a bit at a time. This breathing technique uses a similar principle, where in order to get to the bottom of the exhale, you exhale a bit at a time in a controlled manner. I find this breathing technique to be particularly useful when I am in agitation, fight/flight, or freeze.

Pre-Assessment
Which autonomic state best describes what you feel right now?

- ☐ Calm/connected
- ☐ Vital stress
- ☐ Agitation
- ☐ Fight/flight
- ☐ Freeze
- ☐ Withdrawal

Instructions

1. Find a comfortable position.

2. Inhale as you normally would. Pause briefly at the top of your inhale.

3. Allow some air to slowly "vent" before "catching it" and holding the breath again momentarily.

4. Vent and pause for another three to five increments or until you are at the bottom of the exhale.

5. Inhale again and repeat the incremental "venting" exhale for five cycles.

6. After completing the desired number of breath exhale cycles, allow your breath to return to its natural rhythm. Notice any changes in your heart rate, muscle tension, or overall sense of relaxation.

Post-Assessment
Which autonomic state best describes what you feel right now?

- ☐ Calm/connected
- ☐ Vital stress
- ☐ Agitation
- ☐ Fight/flight
- ☐ Freeze
- ☐ Withdrawal

Describe any changes you noticed in your body, emotions, or thoughts either during or after the exercise.

_____

_____

_____

_____

Five-Minute Experiment

In this exercise, you will experiment with a technique to help your nervous system ease out of its stress response. There are numerous tools that can effect a shift in your body's experience of stress and bring you closer to a calm/connected home base. The key is to be open and use your experience tuning in to your body to notice any shifts.

Below the pre-assessment you'll find a list of suggestions, or you can pick something else that you have in mind. I recommend selecting an activity that you wouldn't normally do.

Pre-Assessment

Which autonomic state best describes what you feel right now?

- [ ] Calm/connected
- [ ] Vital stress
- [ ] Agitation
- [ ] Fight/flight
- [ ] Freeze
- [ ] Withdrawal

Instructions

Suggested experiments that take five minutes or less (choose one):

- [ ] Put a hand over your heart and take three slow breaths
- [ ] Meditate (apps can be helpful—e.g., Insight Timer, Liberate, Headspace)
- [ ] Write down five things you are grateful for
- [ ] Go outside into daylight (with appropriate sun protection for your skin)
- [ ] Put music on and dance to it
- [ ] Hum a tune or chant
- [ ] Gargle water for 20 seconds
- [ ] Listen to soothing music
- [ ] Get a hug that lasts three breaths from someone
- [ ] Drink a cup of herbal tea
- [ ] Other: _____

Post-Assessment

Which autonomic state best describes what you feel right now?

- [ ] Calm/connected
- [ ] Vital stress
- [ ] Agitation
- [ ] Fight/flight
- [ ] Freeze
- [ ] Withdrawal

Describe any changes you noticed in your body, emotions, or thoughts either during or after the exercise.

_____

_____

_____

_____

One-Hour Experiment

In this exercise, you will choose a technique for shifting your autonomic state back to home base that takes an hour or less to do. Because these experiments take longer than the options from the previous exercise, you may have to plan when to do them.

Below the pre-assessment you'll find a list of suggestions, or you can pick something else that you have in mind. I recommend selecting something that you wouldn't normally do.

Pre-Assessment

Which autonomic state best describes what you feel right now?

☐ Calm/connected ☐ Vital stress ☐ Agitation
☐ Fight/flight ☐ Freeze ☐ Withdrawal

Instructions

Suggested experiments that take less than an hour or less (choose one):

☐ Take a warm bath
☐ Practice mindfulness while eating a meal
☐ Take a 20-minute power nap
☐ Take a yoga class (there are many free, short yoga classes on YouTube)
☐ Enjoy coffee or tea with a friend
☐ Engage in a creative activity (draw, paint, write a song, etc.)
☐ Turn off digital devices for an hour in the evening
☐ Walk in nature
☐ Laugh with someone (watch a comedy show, tell jokes, etc.)
☐ Other: _____

Post-Assessment

Which autonomic state best describes what you feel right now?

☐ Calm/connected ☐ Vital stress ☐ Agitation
☐ Fight/flight ☐ Freeze ☐ Withdrawal

Describe any changes you noticed in your body, emotions, or thoughts either during or after the exercise.

_____

_____

_____

_____

Patience and Progress

I hope in this chapter you found at least one tool that made a difference in helping you reset to your calm/connected home base and got some practice with it. Let's address some challenges you may encounter as you practice finding and resetting to home base. The biggest challenge I hear about is frustration when people don't think they are very good at it or when they forget to use these tools when they are triggered.

Try to remember that your conscious mind is not in charge of your body's safety and survival. The part of you that is responsible for this, your nervous system, is uniquely qualified for the job because it can continuously process countless bits of information about the past and present, and then make predictions about the future. When you feel frustration or impatience, try to remember how good your nervous system is at doing its job. Its track record of keeping you alive is stellar! Try to extend compassion to your nervous system and conscious mind, both of which are working hard to do what's best for you.

Also, remember that even small shifts are very worthwhile. Allow yourself to fully appreciate your progress. Even if the shift is only 10 percent of the way toward a fully calm and relaxed state, know that in that 10 percent is still a world where you can build your awareness. It means that your nervous system has responded and you can continue the conversation with it.

I find it so rewarding to work with clients as they start to realize that anxiety and panic are not entirely out of their control. Instead of going into a doom loop of deliberating, analyzing, and ruminating, they start to discover that the key to unlocking a different way of being in the world is in something as simple as redirecting their attention on their body.

You, too, will eventually encounter a time when you will feel overwhelmed or uneasy, and your knowledge about autonomic states and how to guide yourself back to calm/connected will be empowering. It may occur to you that you don't need to change other people or your entire environment to feel more at ease, but you can accomplish the same by doing something as deliberate and doable as taking a few regulating breaths.

It is quite normal to forget about the tools at your disposal when your autonomic state is more activated toward stress and threat. For some people, it just takes more practice. But if you notice that your autonomic dysregulation is chronic despite your best efforts, or that it seems impossible to tune in to your body's signals, then consider that these might be signs of trauma in your nervous system. The next chapter addresses this.

CHAPTER 5

Rewiring Early Trauma

When Eli was three, his brother was born with a medical condition. With Eli's brother needing extra care, his parents were often too tired and busy to give Eli much attention. One evening, Eli wanted to show his mother a drawing he had made, but his mom, exhausted and busy, responded sharply, "Not now!" Eli was shocked and felt collapsed. His parents were too distracted to notice or even take the time to explain what was happening to Eli.

Situations like this kept happening, and his brain made the connection that seeking attention meant getting rejected. Eli's brain flagged his desire to get attention as dangerous. His nervous system helped suppress these urges by triggering internal states that altered his thoughts and actions. If he had to do something on stage for school, he would panic with anxiety. He stopped having urges to share freely about himself with anyone. He easily made friends, but Eli remained pretty reserved in all his relationships.

Parental rejection is a threat of the highest magnitude at that young age, and Eli's experience of it introduced ongoing dysregulation in his nervous system. Without realizing it, Eli's nervous system was constantly defending itself against "unwanted" urges to seek attention and share anything about himself. Within these states of dysregulation, Eli formed a strategy to ignore and suppress his needs for attention. Over time, his nervous system was so effective that Eli didn't know he even had these needs.

Early attachment trauma arises from the threat of losing those who care for us. From birth, our primary instinct for survival is to maintain our lifeline to our caregivers: "If someone is taking care of me, I must stay connected to them and keep them coming back for me!" So, connection is equated with survival, and any perceived risk to this bond can feel as critical as a threat to our life itself. As we explored in chapter 2, trauma can develop from a single overwhelming and unresolved event that prompts the brain to flag things associated with that event as dangerous. If similar events repeat and reinforce these responses, the trauma becomes more deeply ingrained. Contrary to how dramatic the word *trauma* can seem, the things that get flagged as dangerous can be very mundane, like Eli's excitement to seek his parents' attention. So, even though it isn't logical for Eli as a grown adult to be afraid to seek a spotlight of any kind, this old trauma still affects him.

The fact that many of us have these flags from trauma to varying degrees is another piece of the puzzle when it comes to supporting regulation in your nervous system. You can train yourself to find home base, and even perhaps train your nervous system to be more efficient at finding home base, but trauma will disrupt these efforts and send your body into a defense state. Or you might be so constantly triggered by these flags that you struggle to really even identify your home base. This dysregulation not only makes us lose emotional stability; it impacts the body's ability to rest and rejuvenate. It can even affect our body's ability to absorb nutrients from the foods we eat or to clear inflammation, contributing to problems with your physical health.

In this chapter, we'll try to root out some of the common early trauma patterns that can limit us. Knowing what these are helps us understand the triggers that implicitly stress us out. In cultivating this awareness, we can get one step closer to resolving trauma and building a stronger attachment foundation.

Trauma Triggers

Triggers can be anything we experience in the present that our brain has previously flagged as dangerous. Common triggers include having a particular feeling (like anger), someone else having a particular feeling (like a loved one seeming sad), a topic of conversation (like finances), or a kind of relationship interaction (like a disagreement or sharing intimacy). The possibilities are endless. And when we experience these triggers, our body rapidly responds with dysregulation and defense. Oftentimes, this takes the form of a familiar behavior or response. So, it might be agitation and expressing worry. Or it could be panic and blaming or criticizing, or freeze and people-pleasing, or withdrawal and falling asleep.

How can we tell when we (or others) are triggered? Some people are keenly aware of what their triggers are and how they are affected by them. But for those who are naive of their trauma, when they realize something is up with them, they usually explain it with a sentence that begins with, "It feels like . . ." Now, what follows is not usually a feeling, such as sadness or anger. Instead, it is often a narrative that describes a very subjective experience that we can usually trace back to an earlier trauma.

These are all real examples I've heard. "It feels like . . .":

- I'm a joke to you.

- You don't want to hear me.

- Things will never get better.

- You don't even know me.

- I can't trust you.

- You never cared about me.

- You don't think I'm good enough for you.

In my experience, when someone starts an accusation with "It feels like," their brain is usually referencing past trauma. Old memories are being overlaid onto the current situation as if the past is happening in the present. While the conscious mind may have tucked away the original distressing event, it remains vividly imprinted in the defense mechanisms of the nervous system, which remains on high alert for any reminders. Hence, these "it feels like" statements can serve as windows into the underlying trauma.

If you can remember doing this at some point, try not to feel bad about it. All our brains do some version of this. It's the brain's best attempt at putting the pieces together in a moment of distress and dysregulation. Instead, I invite you to be curious when you witness the "it feels like" phenomenon in yourself. Or you can even take advantage of your brain's attempt at associations by asking yourself when you are triggered, *What does it feel like?* Chances are, you will uncover feelings in yourself or actions from others that your brain has flagged as dangerous.

One step you can take in this workbook is to become more aware of the traumas that your nervous system references when it gets triggered. These traumas, whether they are clear memories or not, are creating yellow and red alert moments in your life and in your relationships, sometimes without any real cause other than the fact that they remind your brain of the past.

"It Feels Like" Exploration

The purpose of this exercise is to help you recognize when you may be experiencing a reaction to past traumas and reflect on what early experiences they originate from. Past traumas, especially those linked to early attachment, can subconsciously impact our reactions and perceptions in the present. Understanding and recognizing these moments can be a powerful step toward unhooking yourself from the trauma.

1. Recall a recent event when you experienced a conflict or disappointment in a relationship and felt a strong emotional reaction as a result. Briefly describe what happened.

_____

_____

_____

2. Reflect on the emotional jolt you experienced. What words come to mind to describe it?

_____

_____

_____

3. Try to identify the narrative behind this emotional reaction. (You can refer to the previous examples if needed.) "It feels like . . .":

_____

_____

_____

4. Reflect on the sentence you just completed. Can you identify anyone in your past who also acted similarly or made you feel this way? Try to think back as far as you can, or even make guesses.

_____

_____

_____

5. Given what you've reflected on, do you think your reaction to the recent event was solely based on that event, or might it have been influenced by past traumas? Why or why not?

_____

_____

_____

_____

6. Understanding that our past can influence our reactions, is there a way you would prefer to respond if a similar event happens in the future? What strategies or tools could you employ to ensure your reaction is based on the present, rather than on past traumas?

_____

_____

_____

_____

Trauma and Insecure Attachment

Early trauma is embedded into insecure attachment and disrupts our attachment foundation, or the foundation that allows us to effectively lean on others for support. Insecure attachment strategies in response to stress, like avoiding, protesting, people-pleasing, or shutting down, are hallmarks of defense states. And we know that these patterns form, in part, because they are adaptations to repeated patterns of inconsistent, neglectful, or confusing treatment from our caregivers when we were young.

One version of this for many people with anxious attachment is that their brains flag distancing behaviors from friends and partners as a threat and they find themselves reflexively agitated or fighting for reassurance in ways that work against the connection they seek. Meanwhile, the brains of people with avoidant attachment easily flag intimacy-seeking behaviors from loved ones as threatening to the more stripped-down version of connection that they are familiar with, and they end up automatically withdrawing or fighting these perceived demands.

People with a disorganized attachment style usually had even more terrifying or confusing early attachment experiences, causing more prominent patterns of dysregulation. Their brains might flag any aspect of relating as a threat, even connection itself. Their triggers can be sporadic with specific memories and situations or more constant because they are triggered by more fundamental aspects of relating, like feeling vulnerable or being seen by others.

Even if it isn't obvious, many of us have adaptations that were formed from early attachment trauma. In the next exercise, you'll explore whether you might as well.

Identifying Trauma Adaptations

Early trauma is actually very common, as we've all had experiences that might have been overwhelming when no one was around to help us process them. It's important to be able to recognize the effects these early traumas may continue to have in your life and relationships. In order to practice identifying the early trauma that you may carry with you, let's explore a memory of a difficult experience from early in your life.

1. Think back to a difficult experience you had with a parent or other caregiver when you were a child. What was most challenging about it?

   _____

   _____

   _____

   _____

2. As children, when people fail to effectively meet our needs in a way that soothes our distress and reassures us with connection, we often get the message that there is something wrong or unlovable with us that jeopardizes connection. Considering the memory that you just wrote about, which messages do you think you could have internalized? Check all that apply or list your own.

   Connection is in jeopardy if I:
   - ☐ Take up space
   - ☐ Challenge people
   - ☐ Have different opinions
   - ☐ Am my own person
   - ☐ Am upset or angry
   - ☐ Am dissatisfied
   - ☐ Need help
   - ☐ Want attention
   - ☐ Make mistakes
   - ☐ Fail to meet expectations
   - ☐ Talk about bad things that happened
   - ☐ Have emotional needs

☐ Am sick

☐ Am too independent

☐ Shine too brightly

☐ Do better than others

☐ Other: _____

☐ Other: _____

3. When connection is in jeopardy, we also tend to eventually adapt to preserve any connection that we can. We internalize the idea, *Taking care of me is hard! I must make it easier so I can keep the connection!* What strategies might you have adopted to continue to receive love and connection? Check all that apply or list your own.

To keep the connection, I need to:

☐ Stay out of the way

☐ Be perfect

☐ Be a "good boy" or "good girl"

☐ Stay quiet

☐ Keep the peace

☐ Be happy no matter what

☐ Suppress my emotions

☐ Suppress my needs

☐ Be _____ enough (*Examples: funny, impressive, smart, attractive, nice, sweet, successful*)

☐ Follow along and stay completely loyal

☐ Cheer others up

☐ Be responsible for everything

☐ Take care of everything/everyone

☐ Fight harder for attention

☐ Make others happy

☐ Put myself down

☐ Believe that I'm unlovable

☐ Ignore what is happening

☐ Other: _____

☐ Other: _____

4. Naming these patterns and dynamics gives us the power to recognize them when they show up in how we interact with people in our adult lives. Complete the sentences below to name the adaptation you just explored.

   Connection is in jeopardy if I _____ !

   To keep the connection, I need to _____ !

5. Are there any ways that you see this dynamic showing up in your current relationships? Describe the connections you notice between your past experiences and your present patterns.

   _____

   _____

   _____

   _____

6. Acknowledging our past traumas and their influence on us is difficult work. I encourage you to take some time now to check in with yourself—how are you feeling in your body, heart, and mind? You might like to use the space below to journal about your experience. You may also wish to practice one or more of the exercises from chapter 4 to help you return to your calm/connected home base.

   _____

   _____

   _____

   _____

Releasing Trauma and Getting Help

Our adaptations from early attachment trauma make forming, maintaining, and trouble-shooting relationships that much harder. In Eli's case, his nervous system effectively made him have a blind spot about his need for attention and self-expression, which continued to hamper his ability to show up fully in relationships and ultimately impacted his ability to form deeper bonds.

Being in a state of fight/flight panic may lead you to say things you later regret. Being caught in a freeze state could make you avoid dealing with an important issue that only builds the longer you ignore it. When you are anxious or withdrawn, it's harder to feel connected to the people you love. And this dysregulation causes behaviors like avoidance that perpetuate an insecure attachment style, which almost guarantees more future dysregulation and stress. It's a vicious cycle.

The only way to ensure an end to the cycle is to find a way to release the trauma. Once you manage to release your trauma, there are no longer trip wires in your relationships that set off big and small dysregulation bombs. This frees up your nervous system so it is able to return to calm/connected more easily.

The work of releasing trauma is delicate and requires patience and attunement. It simply doesn't work to dictate when and how this should happen. It needs to be a supportive and respectful process that invites the body to find new mechanisms for feeling safe in place of fearful defense.

The skills you are developing in this book to attune to your nervous system and explore your adaptations to attachment trauma are a good way to prepare for more extensive work to release trauma. This serves as excellent groundwork to develop awareness and steady your focus on the body's signals. As you begin to gain more awareness of your autonomic states, gain facility in bringing your system back to a calm/connected home base, and even practice advanced skills to make your nervous system more efficient at regulating itself, you will be in a good position to work on resolving your trauma responses.

Getting Visceral

When you are ready to do this work, the first step will be to get in touch, on a visceral level, with why your trauma adaptation was so needed. Often this kind of understanding is buried deep within layers and layers of old memories and experiences. It takes time and the right kind of curiosity and attention to excavate these layers and trace the logic of your survival instincts.

At first, exploring your trauma adaptations might feel very abstract, like it may have in the previous exercises. It can sound more like someone else's story than your own. But even exploring trauma on this intellectual level can be a valuable part of the learning process because it makes you curious about your own story in potentially new ways.

You might struggle, for example, with the idea that at some point, losing connection felt like a mortal threat. It might make sense on some theoretical or intellectual level, but you can't *feel* it because it may not be true anymore—you are no longer as reliant on others for survival the way you were when you were a small child. And so, it may be hard to truly feel how behaviors like people-pleasing were strategies to survive. Getting in touch with your trauma and triggers, and eventually healing and releasing them, is about being able to feel these old experiences on an emotional level.

Here's a clue: the most effective way to access the root of a trauma is when you are actively in a state of being triggered, even just mildly. I don't suggest you do anything severe to dysregulate yourself, but simply notice when something has triggered you in real time and be curious about it.

When we find access to the embodied logic of these trauma adaptations, these memories no longer feel abstract or like they are someone else's story. It's often a lightbulb moment when we realize, "I needed to be pleasant because it was so terrifying when Mom's moods were unpredictable; being pleasant was the only way I could be sure of not setting her off!" or "When Dad got that upset, it was so scary—shutting down was the best way to feel safe!" Sometimes, we may find ourselves giving words to experiences that we have never named before.

These might sound like scary realizations. Having a caring and competent therapist or facilitator, as we'll discuss more in a moment, can be invaluable to ensure that you can explore these memories safely without further harm or retraumatization. But when we make these connections in a way that is visceral rather than intellectual, it can be tremendously validating. All of a sudden, our actions and behaviors make sense. The reason for our autonomic dysregulation is evident. These experiences were red alert moments that our nervous system just couldn't ignore, and so for many years it had been doing its job, reliably using its coping mechanisms to keep us safe—treating relationships with authority, for example, as deserving of watchful alertness, or not trusting people who give us compliments—even if those coping methods eventually didn't work that well anymore.

A Window to Rewrite Memory

Making these visceral and emotional connections—feeling those old feelings again—opens up a window for healing and releasing the trauma. This is because when we access these fear memories, they become more pliable for a period of time through a process called *memory reconsolidation*. Research suggests that this window can last from a few minutes up to four hours, depending on a number of factors. During this window, the brain can strengthen, weaken, or modify the memory based on your present experience. You can create the conditions for the brain to create a new memory association during that time by one or both of the following:

1. **Experiencing safety:** Being more regulated and experiencing some degree of safety, or less autonomic defense activation, can help you reshape your memory. What's important here is that your nervous system has to experience cues of safety. This could include being with a safe, nonjudgmental person, calming your body with breathing exercises, practicing self-compassion, or orienting.

2. **Noticing evidence of an alternative:** This involves experiencing compelling evidence that the defense response is not needed as it once was. Take, for example, Natalie, whose nervous system has flagged making mistakes as a threat to connection. If she makes a mistake with her current partner, Liz,

she could really focus her attention on how Liz forgave her, and in fact, being honest about the mistake brought them closer together.

The first item is more important, because often with trauma, simply being in a more regulated state makes it evident to our nervous system that the threat is not as real as it once was. If you try to experience evidence of an alternative without first feeling safe, then the nervous system will not care what the new evidence is. That is because, in order to ensure survival, your nervous system will prioritize any information coming from your autonomic state over your rational brain. Naturally, if you're accessing a traumatic memory, your autonomic state will reflect that old trauma, and you will be dysregulated.

Continuing the example of Natalie, if her body could not reach a more calm/connected state while she told Liz about her mistake, or in the pliable window afterward, then it wouldn't matter that Liz was gracious and forgiving. Natalie could try to reason, *Liz was so good to me! I shouldn't have this trauma response anymore.* But Natalie's nervous system would only have gotten cues of danger from her body, reinforcing the trauma response.

This is yet another example of why learning to help guide your body back to a calm/connected state can be so useful.

The body is absolutely essential in trauma processing. A trained trauma therapist doesn't just listen to the thoughts and emotions that clients consciously express. Instead, we watch for their body's signals—facial expressions, body movements and position, breathing rate, jaw tension, pupil dilation, eye contact, vocal inflections, and other physical clues of their internal experience and autonomic state. Paying close attention to these signals and knowing how to interpret and verify them is how I figure out how to support a client's process. The complexity of the trauma often determines how long it takes to rewire and resolve. Sometimes trauma can be released and reorganized with just a bit of prompting, and other times there are layers and layers of negotiation that happen over years.

Depending on the complexity of the trauma memory, you may need to repeat this process of accessing these memories and experiences several times. Sometimes, after making this visceral connection once and working on it a bit, the connection will fade into the background as you reenter everyday living, until you get triggered or call it back up again. Be prepared to discover and rediscover the trigger.

An experienced trauma professional can help you track your progress and offer tools and strategies at each step of the way to help you negotiate the process of understanding and rewiring your trauma responses. Some professionals work with methods that are more verbal, while others use more body-based methods, but ideally, the professional you work with should understand when and how to use each approach.

Patience and Progress

Processing trauma makes room for your nervous system to live in its calm/connected state more often rather than be caught in states of defense and stay dysregulated. This has many benefits for your mental and physical health. When you address the trauma that limits your ability to rely on others and be your authentic self in relationships, then you also build up a stronger attachment foundation, expanding your ability to be resilient to stress in the world.

As we've discussed before, being able to form secure attachments and being resilient to stress are biologically interwoven. When you can be at ease with supportive people in your life, you have a greater ability to deal with life's challenges and experience a more regulated nervous system.

The tools you've gained so far will give you a great start to addressing trauma by giving you the foundation to listen to your body, help your nervous system find its calm/connected home base, and understand the nervous system's signals in response. Additionally, you may find that you have a better idea of what to look for as you navigate this process and that you can appreciate the value of working with someone who is trained to help you process trauma. With these skills and an attitude of collaboration with—not against—your nervous system, you can feel confident that you've adequately prepared for the journey ahead.

Because healing from trauma requires a significant amount of neuroplasticity and rewiring, the most difficult part can be allowing yourself the time and space to "not know" before your brain and body begin to integrate and make sense of things again. There will be moments when you feel unsteady and have more unanswered questions than when you started. When working on early trauma, we may find ourselves asking questions like:

- Is having this person in my life right for me?

- How can I possibly let my guard down and still feel safe?

- Nothing makes sense. Will it ever?

When you encounter these and other potentially challenging questions, remember to hold this experience with compassion, but also know that it's a sign of progress. You can't get to this stage unless you take the steps to question and address the defenses that shield you from having to ask them. Processing trauma means your nervous system gets support to answer these questions in a new way, on its own timeline. And this can be challenging because it is new.

Taking on the journey to address and heal trauma leads you home to yourself. Early relational traumas usually cling to us and become so familiar that it can take some time to tease them apart. You may wonder, *Who am I without the trauma that dysregulates me?* The next chapter will help you explore this question in more depth.

CHAPTER 6

Feelings, Boundaries, and Desires

In this journey through life, your body and nervous system also give rise to your feelings, boundaries, and desires. These are the constantly evolving markers that make up the core of who you are. Being in touch with these things means that you can know yourself and choose to share them with other people, allowing for true intimacy and connection. But if you live under constant stress or with the dysregulation of trauma, it's not uncommon to lose touch with these core parts of yourself or find them difficult to decipher.

Polyvagal theory informs us that the autonomic state of our bodies determines how we experience ourselves, others, and the world. This includes the sense of, *What do I really feel and want?* If you have ever been confused about this, it may have something to do with the fact that you have been dysregulated. Your autonomic state is like a filter that is overlaid on your experience of feelings, boundaries, and natural desires, and that filter can add urgency to or dull how we perceive ourselves. But when the nervous system can return to safety, and calibrate our bodies for rest and connection, we can put our guard down and identify and explore our feelings, boundaries, and desires in a more authentic way.

Let's consider an example. Adele is someone who identifies herself as having an avoidant attachment style. When she is particularly stressed at work, she usually finds her partner very irritating upon returning home. They normally have dinner together, but this is when Adele gets the strong desire to lock herself in the basement and play video games. This is an example of how prolonged work stress, coupled with attachment stress, can keep someone in a dysregulated state, in this case in what looks like a freeze response. When I ask Adele how she knows she is stressed, she mentions how tight her breath gets, the tension in her belly, and her tendency to say something rude to her partner. Now, there is absolutely nothing wrong with wanting to be alone for a while, but this was not just that. The impulse to want some alone time, in Adele's case, could easily become adversarial due to her pushing away (and being rude to) her partner.

How can we get to the bottom of our authentic feelings, boundaries, and desires when we are agitated, frozen, or numbed out? Let's recall that according to polyvagal theory, we don't get to pick and choose our experience within these states. So, to experience these aspects of our authentic selves, it's necessary to step out of our autonomic defense responses and find our calm/connected home base. We can do this through safe, relatively stress-free relationships, using breath or other practices, or overcoming trauma that gets in the way of regulation.

When it comes to being fulfilled in relationships, it's essential to have access to what you feel and what your boundaries and desires are. When you know these things—or can take the time to figure them out—you can participate in relationships in a way that is authentic and fulfilling. When these things are obscure or confusing to you because you are momentarily, or even perpetually, in a defense state, it's difficult to know your authentic self or let others get to know you.

This is another reason why living in dysregulation can be hard on relationships, and why our lives can run better when we return to a calm/connected state and take the time to listen to our thoughts, feelings, and desires. In this chapter, you'll explore ways to become more aware of your feelings, boundaries, and desires.

Processing Your Emotions

Emotions are sensory experiences that we have from the time we are infants. Yet, as infants and toddlers, these feelings are raw and unprocessed, pulsing through us without a definitive name. It's only as we grow, through invaluable interactions with caregivers, peers, and educators, that we learn to put words to these sensations. By developing a lexicon for our feelings, we provide our rational minds with the tools to categorize, understand, and communicate about our emotions.

A lexicon for feelings is very useful for creating deep bonds with others. The willingness to express your emotions—and recognize that others have them too—is essential to building these connections. It shapes the foundation of understanding and empathy, which are fundamentals for strong relationships. However, the importance of naming feelings hasn't always been emphasized or understood in our society and culture. Many people, whether due to cultural norms, trauma, or other challenges, find it difficult to understand emotions and articulate them.

What do we do with feelings? First, we need to genuinely experience our feelings, being present with them as they move through our bodies. Second, and crucially, we must learn to name them. Naming feelings has been shown to be an effective way to decrease the intensity of negative feelings, and it may even enhance the joy from positive ones. The following exercises are designed to guide you in feeling and naming your emotions, going from raw sensory experience to a more nuanced understanding of what you are feeling.

Naming Emotions

Emotions are the way our bodies and brains respond to what's going on around us; they're signals that give us a lot of information about ourselves and our situations. If we pay attention to them, they can help us navigate our lives. If we have trouble understanding our emotions, we may have a harder time making good decisions or dealing in a healthy way with what's going on. The purpose of this exercise is to explore different events in the past and the emotions that accompanied them.

I'll ask you to recall a scenario that you have likely experienced and to (1) identify the body sensations that you feel when you think about what happened, and (2) name three emotions you experienced and why you think you may have experienced them. Practicing this as often as possible is a great way to gain more emotional intelligence. To that end, I've left the final scenario blank for you to fill in—you can make copies of that page to use in your future practice.

Scenario 1

Recall a time when someone you knew was very sick (this could be a person or a pet).

1. Describe the incident. (Who was sick? What was your relationship to them? What happened?)

_____

_____

_____

2. Recalling it now, what sensations are you experiencing in your body? (This can be very general, such as tightness in upper body, or more specific, such as cold, tight restriction in the throat.)

_____

_____

_____

3. Complete the sentences below to describe your emotions during that incident. You can reference some possible emotions in the chart that follows. (Example: I felt <u>concerned</u> because <u>my dog was in pain.</u>)

    a. I felt _____ because _____.

    b. I felt _____ because _____.

    c. I felt _____ because _____.

Consider the following options to help you get started:			
• Sad	• Dread	• Helpless	• Overwhelmed
• Afraid	• Angry	• Shock	• Resigned
• Worried	• Frustrated	• Despair	• Hopeful
• Anxious	• Guilty	• Lonely	• Confused

Scenario 2

Recall a time you watched a sunset.

1. Describe the incident. (Where were you? Were you with anyone?)

    _____

    _____

    _____

2. Recalling it now, what sensations are you experiencing in your body? (This can be very general, such as stillness in your body, or more specific, such your breath becoming slow and deep.)

    _____

    _____

    _____

3. Complete the sentences below to describe your emotions during that incident. You can reference some possible emotions in the chart that follows. (Example: I felt _wonder_ because _the colors were so beautiful._)

a. I felt _____ because _____.

b. I felt _____ because _____.

c. I felt _____ because _____.

Consider the following options to help you get started:			
• Calm	• Joy	• Solitude	• Curious
• Wonder	• Melancholy	• Inspiration	• Blissful
• Awe	• Serene	• Humility	• Amused
• Contentment	• Gratitude	• Relaxed	• Nostalgic

Scenario 3

Recall a time you received a thoughtful gift from a loved one.

1. Describe the incident. (What was the gift? Who gave it to you? What was it for?)

_____

_____

_____

2. Recalling it now, what sensations are you experiencing in your body? (This can be very general, such as a feeling of warmth, or more specific, such as your face moving into a smile.)

_____

_____

_____

3. Complete the sentences below to describe your emotions during that incident. You can reference some possible emotions in the chart that follows. (Example: I felt <u>excited</u> because <u>I couldn't wait to use the gift.</u>)

a. I felt _____ because _____.

b. I felt _____ because _____.

c. I felt _____ because _____.

Consider the following options to help you get started:			
• Grateful	• Cherished	• Admiring	• Respected
• Appreciated	• Delighted	• Comforted	• Proud
• Surprised	• Content	• Connected	• Touched
• Excited	• Fulfilled	• Validated	• Secure

Scenario 4

Recall a time someone wouldn't listen to something important you had to say.

1. Describe the incident. (Who would not listen? What were you trying to tell them?)

_____

_____

_____

2. Recalling it now, what sensations are you experiencing in your body? (This can be very general, such as feeling detached from your body, or more specific, such as light-headedness and ringing in your ears.)

_____

_____

_____

3. Complete the sentences below to describe your emotions during that incident. You can reference some possible emotions in the chart that follows. (Example: I felt _angry_ because _I felt disrespected._)

a. I felt _____ because _____.

b. I felt _____ because _____.

c. I felt _____ because _____.

Consider the following options to help you get started:			
• Frustrated	• Confused	• Disappointed	• Hopeless
• Annoyed	• Rejected	• Anxious	• Resigned
• Sad	• Resentful	• Embarrassed	• Humiliated
• Angry	• Hurt	• Inadequate	• Betrayed

Scenario 5

Choose your own scenario: _____

1. Describe the incident.

_____

_____

_____

2. Recalling it now, what sensations are you experiencing in your body?

_____

_____

_____

3. Complete the sentences below to describe your emotions during that incident.

a. I felt _____ because _____.

b. I felt _____ because _____.

c. I felt _____ because _____.

Emotions vs. Autonomic State

I mentioned earlier that emotions are not the same as autonomic state. This can be a confusing idea because in everyday speech, we tend to collapse and confound states with emotions. For example, people commonly refer to panic and anxiety as feelings when what they feel is in fact influenced greatly by their autonomic state.

Defense states that are governed by high levels of the alertness system (i.e., agitation and fight/flight) instill panic and pump up the intensity of emotions, making people act in ways that are rigid and demanding. Historically, this has been used to give emotions a bad rap, making people believe that emotions are what make us lose control and act irrationally. This belief leads people to distrust emotions, including their own.

However, experiencing intense emotions does not automatically mean that we will be dysregulated. How we experience an emotion will change depending on our autonomic state, but it is possible to experience just about any emotion in a regulated way—that is, a way that is mainly anchored to the calm/connected state. When we process the trauma or stress that dysregulates us, we actually get to experience our emotions in this way.

I'll give you an example. When I began working with Lily, she avoided her emotions, which was sensible because they were so dysregulating for her. This turned out to be a result of early trauma, which trained her to avoid feelings like anger or sadness because these emotions garnered so much disapproval in her family. When Lily would try to venture into feeling these emotions as an adult, her trauma predictably would pull her into panic and defense. It was so intense that it felt like life or death to her. Honestly, it was very intense to sit with for me as well. Lily's nervous system fought hard against her efforts to feel her emotions rather than ignore or suppress them. At times, our sessions looked like something out of an exorcism scene, and afterward Lily reported that it felt like she had just had an exhausting workout.

One day, after we had worked together to create the conditions for her to feel her emotions and integrate them, she described an experience of sadness and longing with tears and sorrow. "There goes my dysregulation again," she quipped. I pointed out to her that this looked very different from her panic state and that the expression I saw matched the feelings she was describing. She slowly accepted this and realized that, for the first time, she was able to feel sadness just as it was, without the jolt of survival stress—the old protective response—she used to experience. The feeling was intense, but vital.

Emotions aren't the problem when it comes to dysregulation or trauma. In fact, having emotions that you can feel is a sign of health and wellness. Furthermore, we want to be able to feel them and still return to a calm/connected state because this actually allows us to integrate these emotions and let them guide our interests and decisions in life.

There are many "feelings" lists out there that help us expand our lexicon so that we can find the right word for the range of our internal emotional states. I've put together the following one, which lists a number of feelings that are color coded to the autonomic states in which they are commonly felt. Some of these feelings only span one or two different autonomic states. Others, like vulnerable or sad, can be felt in many more states because it's somewhat common for our nervous systems to flag these feelings as dangerous, and so feeling them automatically can provoke our bodies into an autonomic defense response.

Feelings Chart with Autonomic States

Calm/ Connected	Vital Stress	Agitation	Fight/Flight	Freeze	Withdrawal
Peaceful					
Content					
Tender					
Accepted					
Accepting					
Curious					
Grateful					
Hopeful					
Joyful					
Playful					
Respected					
Safe					
Remorseful					
Caring					
Sad					
Vulnerable					
	Awestruck				

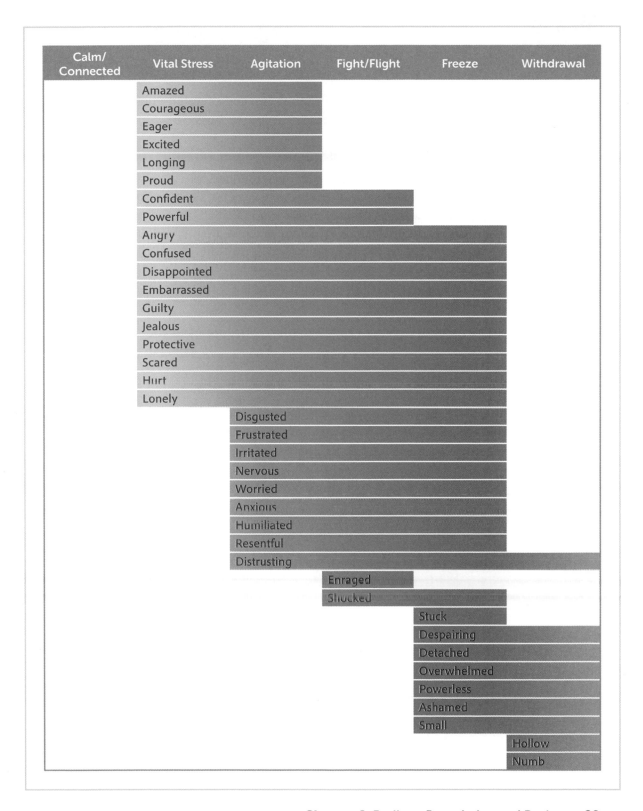

Calm/Connected	Vital Stress	Agitation	Fight/Flight	Freeze	Withdrawal
	Amazed				
	Courageous				
	Eager				
	Excited				
	Longing				
	Proud				
	Confident	←			
	Powerful	←			
	Angry	←	←	←	
	Confused	←	←	←	
	Disappointed	←	←	←	
	Embarrassed	←	←	←	
	Guilty	←	←	←	
	Jealous	←	←	←	
	Protective	←	←	←	
	Scared	←	←	←	
	Hurt	←	←	←	
	Lonely	←	←	←	
		Disgusted	←	←	
		Frustrated	←	←	
		Irritated	←	←	
		Nervous	←	←	
		Worried	←	←	
		Anxious	←	←	
		Humiliated	←	←	
		Resentful	←	←	
		Distrusting	←	←	←
			Enraged		
			Shocked	←	
				Stuck	
				Despairing	←
				Detached	←
				Overwhelmed	←
				Powerless	←
				Ashamed	←
				Small	←
					Hollow
					Numb

Emotions vs. Autonomic State

Now it's your turn to explore your feelings in the landscape of autonomic states. On the following page, you will see a chart with a list of 30 different feelings.

Instructions

1. Read each feeling word to yourself, either silently or out loud, and allow yourself to feel it in the current moment. You may have to remind yourself of a time you had this feeling or give yourself a hypothetical scenario.

2. Notice the immediate responses in your breathing, heart rate, muscle tension, mental activity, and vigilance level.

3. Make a quick guess about the autonomic state that this feeling evokes right now.

4. Put a check mark along the colored spectrum that corresponds to your guess. (Note: full shutdown is left out of the list because emotions are only detectable when you are conscious.)

Reflection

You have a formidable claim to being emotionally intelligent when you can experience your emotions and stay regulated—that is, be able to experience them in a calm/connected state, or return to such a state quickly. Many of us are still working toward this goal with certain emotions. Use the space below to reflect on which feelings are particularly dysregulating for you. You could write about why this could be the case or imagine what it would be like to experience them in a more regulated way. Refer to the Feelings Chart on p. 98 if it is useful.

_____

_____

_____

_____

	Calm/ Connected	Vital Stress	Agitation	Fight/ Flight	Freeze	Withdrawal
Accepted						
Curious						
Grateful						
Playful						
Safe						
Remorseful						
Sad						
Vulnerable						
Longing						
Proud						
Powerful						
Angry						
Confused						
Disappointed						
Embarrassed						
Guilty						
Jealous						
Scared						
Lonely						
Frustrated						
Worried						
Resentful						
Enraged						
Stuck						
Despairing						
Overwhelmed						
Powerless						
Ashamed						
Small						
Numb						

Clarifying Your Boundaries

The topic of boundaries can be complex and confusing, so let's try to explain it simply. Boundaries maintain integrity by determining what can pass in and out. Boundaries exist in nature and are intrinsic to natural systems. For example, our cells have membranes that define where the cell begins and ends. Your skin is also a natural boundary. When it is healthy, it protects your internal body from the external world, but if you have a cut, it can allow bacteria in and the cut can get infected. That's why we bandage wounds on our skin—to keep the boundary protected.

It's also natural for you as a sentient being to have emotional and psychological boundaries as a means of keeping safe and ensuring the integrity of your authentic self. Emotional and psychological boundaries acknowledge that you need to protect yourself beyond your physical body. The old adage "Sticks and stones can break my bones, but words can never hurt me" doesn't apply here. Our openness and interdependence on people can give us joy but can also make us vulnerable to being harmed, and we have a responsibility to protect ourselves to the best of our ability.

Imagine that beyond your skin, you have a strong but invisible bubble around you. Inside this bubble is everything important that makes you, *you*. It includes your feelings, needs, hopes, dreams, preferences, and so on. It even includes your imperfections, like the fact that you can make mistakes. Imagine filling the bubble to its edge with the fullness of who you are. Take a moment, imagine it, and enjoy filling this space with all that is *you*.

Your job is to live life remembering that this bubble exists and knowing why the things inside this bubble are important to you. You then want to cultivate some sensitivity to how external people and events affect you and that bubble. For example, if you're spending time with your friends and a particular friend wants to challenge your beliefs on politics or current events, it's up to you to really consider whether that is welcome. Sometimes your desire to connect, learn, or be challenged will make this a resounding yes. And other times, your internal state, their condescending approach, or something else will make this a clear no.

At the end of the day, you are responsible for maintaining your boundaries and the integrity of what's inside the bubble, not others. Let's say you tell your friend that you aren't up for discussing politics right now, but they insist and continue to barrage you with their thoughts and ideas. You notice the emotional temperature inside you quickly rising, and you don't see any outcome that you would make you want to participate in this conversation. Your friend's actions may be rude and insensitive, but it is your response that will ultimately determine whether the integrity of your bubble is maintained. It's up to you to decide what course of action will best ensure, or restore, the integrity of your bubble.

Then, you must take action. You could decide to say, "Hey, listen, I'm really not up for this discussion. If you need to talk about this right now, I'll just leave the room." This kind of assertiveness acknowledges that you can't control the other person's actions but makes it clear how you can still protect your psychological and emotional boundaries.

If you detect the discomfort and alarm you feel inside, but continue to politely participate in the conversation, this is how that invisible bubble gets breached. It's easy to rationalize that there is little harm in enduring the conversation. Many people do, especially if confrontation makes them uncomfortable or they've had negative experiences with confrontation that have left them scarred.

But the consequences of ignoring your discomfort may be more than you realize. A pattern of this can add up to resentment or lashing at the other person, ultimately eroding your relationship with them. Internalizing stress and avoiding confrontation can set you up for more anxiety and dysregulation in the future. Additionally, the stress of holding things in can be toxic. In his book *When the Body Says No*, Dr. Gabor Maté makes the connection that his patients who develop chronic and serious illnesses are often people who suppress their internal reactions and have a difficult time saying no.

Contrary to what you may have been led to believe by your family of origin or others, maintaining our own boundaries is not other people's responsibility. For the sake of our health and well-being, we need to take charge of how and when we make ourselves available to others. Learning to be very clear in understanding and articulating our boundaries allows us to do this with more ease.

Circle of Care

This exercise will help you recognize what aspects of yourself are important and worthy of protecting by looking at key areas of personal boundary setting.

Instructions

1. The following is a list of areas that many people feel are important for establishing boundaries. Please note, not all of these may be important to you, and some may not feel entirely within your control. Rate each item on a scale of importance to you from 1 to 3, where 1 = very important, 2 = important, and 3 = minimally or not important.

   _____ **Personal space:** *Able to take up physical space and enjoy time alone*

   _____ **Emotions:** *Allow myself to feel and express emotions without judgment or excess influence from how others feel*

   _____ **Time:** *Able to decide who and what gets my time, including work, social engagements, time on digital platforms, and personal time*

   _____ **Energy:** *Able to put limits on my mental and emotional energy and to rest when I need to so I don't burn out*

   _____ **Property:** *Autonomy to decide how to spend or share the resources and money I have*

   _____ **Expression:** *Able to decide how to present myself, my ideas, and creativity*

   _____ **Physical body:** *Able to know and define my body's experience of pleasure, discomfort, and safety*

   _____ **Peace:** *Able to guard against negative influences or stressful environments*

   _____ **Health:** *Freedom to decide my medical treatments and how best to take care of myself, including exercise and diet*

   _____ **Goals:** *Able to define my own goals and my idea of success or fulfillment*

   _____ **Desires:** *Able to define what I want and prioritize this over others' demands and expectations*

   _____ **Flaws:** *Permission to embrace my imperfection and learn from my mistakes*

   _____ **Integrity:** *Able to act without compromising my core beliefs and values*

   _____ **Relationships:** *Able to decide who is important to me and whom to be close or in contact with*

   _____ **Privacy:** *Power to decide when I share things about myself and whom to share with*

2. Review the items you rated as 1 or 2 from the previous list and use this list to figure out at least 8 to 10 things that are crucial for your well-being and happiness (e.g., "my career as a union organizer" or "my relationship with my son"). Include anything that is worth protecting for you. Write these around the figure below, which represents you.

3. Now, draw a boundary circle that encloses you with the items that are essential to you. Let this bubble represent the boundary you set for yourself—it protects the things that matter to you and manages the integrity of your authentic being.

4. What are things that come up as challenges or threats to these essentials? Go back and write a few of them outside of the circle (e.g., "my parents' opinions about my chosen career" or "work expects me to do overtime").

5. Once you've written everything down, take a step back and look at your boundary bubble. What's important here is to realize that even if something doesn't harm your physical body, it may still negatively impact the things that are important to you and the things that make you feel whole.

Reflection

1. Do you think that you generally do a good job of protecting the things that are important to you? Why or why not?

_____

_____

_____

_____

2. Which areas would you like to do a better job of protecting with more effective boundary setting?

_____

_____

_____

_____

3. What are some ideas you have for how to do that?

_____

_____

_____

_____

Articulating Your Boundaries

Boundaries may be natural, but they aren't always easy to articulate. So please don't feel bad if you've ever been confused or had trouble articulating your boundaries. Being able to speak your boundaries clearly can make you a better advocate for the things that are important to you, especially when your body's cues for your boundaries are very subtle or can come out in very pronounced fight/flight reactions.

I don't necessarily mean articulating your boundaries to other people. Articulating your boundaries to yourself is even more important, because these then become the rules and conditions that you live by in order to protect your mental, psychological, and physical regulation and safety. Being aware of your boundaries can be powerful because once you are clear about what they are, you can get creative and flexible with how you protect them, even well before a situation or someone's behavior triggers a reaction from you.

Articulating a boundary involves three parts:

1. **Identifying what's at stake:** What behaviors, feelings, types of support, and experiences are important to you, and how do these serve you? This can be based on your personal values, needs, commitments, and so forth—the things that are important to you and that help you live the life you want (e.g., sleeping eight hours a night keeps me in good health).

2. **Recognizing potential threats:** Who or what may pose a threat to the experiences, behaviors, and goals you want in your life and how (e.g., social engagements that keep me up late)?

3. **Deciding on a course of action:** What actions or steps will you take to hold the boundary? Ideally, taking this step restores you to calm/connected (e.g., I will decline invitations that would keep me up past 10 p.m. unless I can sleep in the next day).

Consider the following examples of putting a boundary into words:

- It's essential that my partner and I support each other as parents and protect the parenting choices we've made together. So, when my mother undermines or criticizes these decisions, we will stick up for each other or give her less access to us and the baby.

- I value the ability to stay regulated in my autonomic state. When a conflict with someone escalates to the point of jeopardizing this, I will extricate myself from the conversation.

- It's important to me to be able to share myself emotionally with a partner. If they show a repeated pattern of breaking our agreements, especially important ones, then I have to put more distance between us and rethink my commitment.

Discovering Your Boundaries Worksheet

1. Recall a recent time in your life when a boundary of yours was compromised and it felt bad to you. (Example: *Last week my friend showed up half an hour late to our lunch and made me miss yoga class.*)

   _____

   _____

   _____

   _____

2. How did your body feel when this happened? (Example: *I felt my heart race and my stomach turn.*)

   _____

   _____

   _____

   _____

3. What was at stake when this boundary was compromised? What did you feel and why? (Example: *I felt disappointed because going to yoga class makes a big difference in my mental health.*)

   I felt _____ because _____

   _____.

4. What was your autonomic state when this happened?
   - ☐ Calm/connected
   - ☐ Vital stress
   - ☐ Agitation
   - ☐ Fight/flight
   - ☐ Freeze
   - ☐ Withdrawal

5. What are some actions you could have taken to adjust your environment or set limits with the other person to restore yourself to a calm/connected state (or to get closer to calm/connected)? (Example: I could have explained to my friend that I could only stay for half an hour for an appetizer because I had to get to my yoga class.)

_____

_____

_____

_____

6. Now, give it your best shot to articulate the boundary that is relevant to you in this scenario. (Example: I care deeply about protecting the structured time I schedule to move my body. If other plans encroach on this time, I will either excuse myself or schedule another class for myself.)

_____

_____

_____

_____

Noticing Your Desires

Desires are innate nudges that connect us to a longing. They can be needs, wants, or preferences, varying in intensity from subtle whispers to roaring calls to action. Like feelings and boundaries, we can also feel these urges through our body. While feelings are often reactions to situations, and we feel boundaries through sensing the body's "no" in response to something, desires can be more proactive, guiding us toward something that is a "yes" for the body in a given moment.

However, these natural instincts can become overshadowed, particularly with trauma or significant stress, which includes insecure attachment. Sometimes it can be difficult to tell the difference between what we really want and need and something that we reach for because we are dysregulated and looking for relief. Sometimes, they can be one and the same.

For example, with avoidant attachment stress, we may genuinely crave some distance in a relationship, but an avoidant attachment style will make this more stressful, and while entranced in a defense state, we will retreat away from others in a way that erodes the relationship, such as "ghosting" someone who has reached out to us because we felt overwhelmed and couldn't deal with telling them what we needed.

On the other hand, we may genuinely crave some connection and assurance, but the dysregulation of anxious attachment may cause us to text someone multiple times when we don't hear from them, making it less likely that we'll get that connection we wanted. Early trauma can also cause us to suppress our natural desires—to reach out to a friend when we're feeling sad, for instance—in order to avoid disapproval, pain, or loss.

Being connected to and following our desires also helps us make decisions. I'm not talking about making impulsive decisions, either! You can feel an impulse to change your career and use it as a sign to investigate further and be strategic rather than acting immediately on the idea. Life is full of decisions to make. Listening to our desires can lead us to more and more satisfying decisions. We can pursue facts and rational information to make pro/con lists. But after looking at all the information available about the decision, it's usually our gut instincts that tell us which option is the right one. When we lose connection to our desires, it's hard to trust ourselves or make decisions that we feel confident about.

Noticing desires means recognizing the signals in your body. They can be strong, like a deep yearning to change careers, or subtle, like an inclination to try a new route during your drive home from work. As we cultivate a sense of safety and return more frequently to a calm/connected state, space emerges for our desires to breathe and grow, and for us to pursue them.

Guided Visualization

In this quick meditation, you'll explore what it's like in your body to feel a desire or impulse. The visualization will work best if you close your eyes. You can go to y.gy/guide or use the QR code to access the recording. Alternatively, you can record the instructions in advance and play them back to yourself or have someone read them to you.

Instructions

1. Begin by taking three slow breaths, extending the exhale and releasing any tension in your forehead, then your jaw, your shoulders, your belly, and finally, the pelvic floor.

2. Close your eyes and picture yourself standing on a tranquil path. Ahead of you, the path splits into two directions, left and right, forming a crossroads.

3. Notice the environment around this crossroads. What's the weather like? Are there trees, mountains, or perhaps water bodies nearby? Take a moment to appreciate it.

4. Take a look at the left-side path. If you have trouble seeing it, then turn your head slightly to the left and continue to imagine the left-side path. Turn your attention to your body and notice how your body responds to this path.

5. Now, turn your head and look toward the right-side path. Check and see how your body responds to this direction.

6. Now sense your desires guiding you, either pulling you toward one direction or the other. Take the time to quiet your mind if needed, and go back and forth between the two directions if it's helpful.

7. You will likely sense an impulse—a pull or a nudge—guiding you toward one of the paths. Don't judge or analyze this impulse. Just allow yourself to feel it and acknowledge it.

8. Imagine yourself walking toward the path that your impulse is guiding you to. Notice what it feels like to listen to your desire to choose a path and then walk that path. How does your chest feel? What do you feel in your stomach? Are there tingles, warmth, or any other sensations elsewhere?

Reflection

How did the impulse show up in your body?

_____

_____

_____

_____

Remember, the aim of this exercise is not to judge or criticize but to develop an understanding. The more you practice, the better you will get at recognizing and understanding your desires.

Finding Comfort in the Body

Even as you read this book, your body may have other needs or desires. Your body works tirelessly to get you through your day, and it appreciates small adjustments that make it more comfortable.

1. First make note of your current autonomic state:

   ☐ Calm/connected   ☐ Vital stress   ☐ Agitation
   ☐ Fight/flight   ☐ Freeze   ☐ Withdrawal

2. Ask your body what it most needs right now to be comfortable. You may feel the urge to empty your bladder, take a sip of water, or eat a snack. Your body may benefit from a stretch, or you may feel a pinch or cramp that will feel better once adjusted. Or your breath may be locked, and you may want a moment to reset to home base. What does your body most need or want right now?

   _____

   _____

   _____

3. If it's possible, mindfully do this for your body.

4. What feels different after following your impulse?

   _____

   _____

   _____

Patience and Progress

Simply by living life, you will experience emotions and desires every day. Particularly in new situations or when something in your life changes, you will probably come into contact with body sensations that alert you to your boundaries. These are all good reasons to check in with your body in order to cultivate a relationship with your instincts and build a solid sense of self. Doing so will help you relate more authentically to others and align yourself with people in the world who can support you.

Also, while the goal is to grow self-awareness of your feelings, boundaries, and desires to make better decisions for yourself and stay in your calm/connected home base, please don't fret if you're not fully there yet. Making check-ins with yourself a regular habit is more important than being perfectly regulated all the time.

Learning to feel your emotions and name them, clarify your boundaries, and follow your desires can be a long journey. Allow yourself to make slow progress. Sometimes, you may try to check in on how you feel, what your boundaries are, and what you want, but you still won't clearly know. It's okay to keep the question open-ended and continue checking in with yourself with curiosity throughout the next week or month. It's better to gently return to the question with yourself than try to squeeze an answer out before your body is ready to give one.

With time and consistent effort, the fruits of this practice become evident. You'll be more emotionally intelligent, paving the way for increased self-trust. You may notice that naming your feelings, recognizing your boundaries, and following your desires blend more seamlessly into your natural responses, enabling you to handle situations more effectively in the moment. As you trust and act on your instincts, life becomes more joyful.

Additionally, by consistently paying attention to your autonomic state and your needs and experiences in the moment, you will rewire your brain, reinforcing the notion that your feelings, emotions, and boundaries matter—and, therefore, you matter. Recognizing and valuing your worth is not selfish; allowing yourself to be known in these ways is what forms the foundation for genuine relationships and connections. Living in dysregulation and defense states creates distortions and blocks us from self-awareness and the ability to share ourselves in intimacy and connection.

The importance of checking in with our feelings, boundaries, and desires will continue as a theme in the upcoming chapters. The next section will help you put everything you have learned together and will introduce skills and tools you can use to bring yourself into safety and connection with others, even when there's conflict or stress.

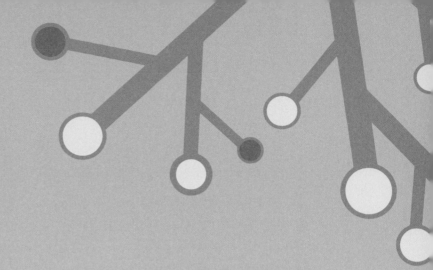

PART III

Creating Connection

Welcome to the final section of this workbook. Having journeyed through understanding the role of stress in relationships, supporting a return to a calm/connected state in your nervous system, and becoming more self-aware, you are now ready to dive into the heart of relationships: connection. The emphasis in these next few chapters is on the vital skills humans need in order to establish deep bonds built on autonomic safety.

You might ask, "Isn't there more to relationships than just safety? What about love or teamwork?" These are certainly important. But understand that from a polyvagal perspective, safety underpins all these other elements we want from a relationship. When safety is compromised on an autonomic level, connecting, collaborating, or even loving becomes a challenging affair. Safety isn't just avoiding threats—it's fostering an environment where we can be genuine and form meaningful connections without fear. It might not always be a sexy topic, but its significance in our relationships is hard to overstate.

Imagine a man and a woman going on a date together. Everything is going well. But then, unknowingly, the man makes a comment that creeps the woman out. In a society where women live with a greater chance that violence will be perpetrated against them by men, she now has her guard up. She politely finishes the date because she doesn't want to offend the man, but she no longer feels safe connecting with him and declines a second date.

Autonomic safety is crucial not only in romantic encounters, but in all types of relationships, including in our workplaces. Google's research of hundreds of teams revealed that the most innovative and collaborative teams were those where members felt safe enough to voice opinions and take risks without fear of ridicule or punishment. In teams without that underlying safety, there was hesitancy, suppression of ideas, and a reluctance to fully participate.

To achieve a deep connection, two critical elements must be present: each person must feel both safe and seen. Coregulation, which we learned about in chapter 1 and will continue to explore in the upcoming chapters, happens when there is enough attentiveness and reassurance in relationships to keep our defensive states at bay. Individuals with a strong attachment foundation developed early in life are often good at coregulation. However, this isn't guaranteed, and it also isn't reserved for those who were fortunate enough to have attentive caregivers. Anyone can develop the skills and practices that nurture interpersonal safety and connection, regardless of their current attachment style.

In the following chapters, we'll explore what it takes to feel seen and to see others. Chapter 7 focuses on what you can do in a relationship to feel safe and seen, chapter 8 describes how you can effectively make others feel safe and seen, and chapter 9 gives you practical tips and advice on how you can stay connected through conflict.

CHAPTER 7

Forging Connection

Rob shared with his friend Hailey that he didn't feel appreciated at work and was thinking about leaving. Hailey knew what an awful economy it was at the moment to job search, and she didn't want him to go through that, so she began to suggest things he could do to make things better in his current position. Rob became tense and guarded. He raised his voice and said, "I've already done those things."

Seeing that Rob was becoming defensive, Hailey took a step back and realized that her own anxiety was leading her response. After taking a moment to reset herself, she explained, "I just realized I didn't give you a chance to talk. I want to hear how it has been for you at work." She gave him space to express his frustrations and fears, asking questions and listening without interrupting. When he finished, she reflected how he felt and validated his concerns—"That sounds so stressful! It makes sense that you're frustrated." Rob softened and looked at his friend with a sigh of relief. Someone understood what he was going through.

Hailey was also glad she took the opportunity to listen and ask questions, as it helped her better understand what was going on with Rob. She did still think there were other ways Rob could try to improve the situation at his current workplace, but this time she brought it up in a more respectful way: "I'll support whatever decision you make, but I have a thought about an option you could consider. Are you open to hearing it?" Rob agreed. Hailey told him her suggestion and at the same time continued to scan the comfort level he was displaying in his facial expressions and body language as she talked. He continued to remain receptive, and even asked her clarifying questions. At the end, Rob thanked Hailey for listening and helping him.

This story is an example of coregulation. Early in the interaction, both Hailey and Rob were in anxiety and defense states. This led them further away from prosocial engagement and being able to connect. In order to return to connection, Hailey intentionally steadied herself and oriented herself toward ways of engaging that would help Rob's nervous system feel safer. Then she was able to help him feel heard. And, even though Hailey appears more active in managing the interaction and turning things around, it also took vulnerable sharing and engagement from Rob to let her know that he trusted her. The two of them managed to collaborate to create a heartwarming interaction that helped them both to feel more connected.

Prioritizing safety and connection can help you forge trust and deeper connections. Taking this approach means helping each person stay in a calm/connected state or quickly return to that home base when triggered. Notice that Hailey did not keep doubling down on her concerns after she noticed that Rob didn't take well to her advice. Insisting on problem-solving in that moment would have come at the expense of connection and safety. Instead, Hailey made a choice to sideline her opinions and recover from what was starting to become a tense moment. In the end, she was still able to give her input, but she only did so after allowing Rob's nervous system to come back to a calm/connected state. She also continued to pay attention to his body language in case there were signs of reactivity that could lead them away from feeling safe with each other again.

Being intentional about coregulation means always having a finger on the pulse of autonomic state—both your own and those of the people you are interacting with. At first, it can seem like a lot of work to continuously check and respond to these autonomic states. Remember, just like anything else, this will become more natural with practice. The benefit is that your relationships will become sources of connection rather than strife.

This chapter gives you frameworks and tools to help you offer care to those around you. Specifically, we'll look at three domains: how to make people feel safe, how to make people feel seen, and a foundational communication tool for collaboration.

Conveying Safety Beyond Words

Have you ever felt truly safe and at ease with someone, even without them uttering a single word? That's the power of coregulation. When two people coregulate, they use touch, eye contact, and sounds in a way that makes each of them feel safe. Coregulation creates a space where everyone can stay grounded in their autonomic home base, which makes connection and collaboration possible.

Words and their meaning are not the most important aspects of coregulation. In fact, the things we say can stir up conflict even when we don't mean them to. Recall the earlier story with Rob and Hailey. Hailey meant no harm when she gave advice to Rob. But her words had the unintended effect of making him feel less connected and safe. The friends' recovery had more to do with each person's nonverbal cues than it had to do with the meaning of their words. Hailey's ability to listen intently, to express curiosity with calm openness, and to cultivate a soft, nonthreatening gaze were more powerful than the words she used.

Nonverbal communication lets another person's nervous system know that it's okay to let its guard down, that it's safe enough to connect in the first place. As with a lot of the techniques I've covered in previous chapters for regulating your autonomic state, what puts your nervous system at ease isn't what you *tell* yourself and whether it is logical; it has more to do with what you *do* to let your body know that it's okay to be in a state of safety. And when you feel safe, those around you are also more likely to feel safe.

Coregulation works best when you use your facial expressions, touch, and vocal intonations to let the other person's nervous system know that it's okay to feel safe and to connect. From the polyvagal perspective, your face and voice are instruments that affect other people (and yourself) in profound ways. When your nervous system senses safety, the prosocial system uses these instruments to play friendly, inviting music that others will usually respond to in kind.

But when you are feeling unsafe or disconnected, the instrument plays ominous, disconcerting music—sometimes called "shark music," after the famously suspenseful score of the film *Jaws*—which is likely to put people on edge and make their nervous systems more vigilant. Others, in turn, broadcast their own autonomic states back to you. Nonverbal signals are really powerful in this way and are key to coregulation and connection.

If you are trying to comfort someone and help them to feel safe, there are a variety of supportive words you can offer, as long as those words are broadcast in a friendly tone. Or you can say nothing at all and simply be present with a soft gaze, a warm smile, and open body language. In either case, the other person's nervous system can directly "hear" these signals your nervous system is broadcasting. Your nervous systems directly communicate with and affect each other.

So, do you just make yourself smile or look friendly? A forced smile seldom looks natural. You might be able to fool someone for a little while, but if the rest of your nonverbal cues don't go along with it, then the lack of congruency can actually be unsettling to the other person and make them feel less safe. Have you ever sensed that someone was anxious and was putting on a smile that looked nervous or frozen? How did you feel around this person? I'm guessing probably not fully at ease.

How *do* you comfort someone or assure them that you are friendly and safe? One way is by making sure—before you engage—that you can find your own autonomic home base, like tuning the instruments in your own nervous system beforehand. Take a calming breath. Stretch your neck and shoulders so that they relax. Gently blink as you look at the other person.

Doing these things with your body can lower your overall defense activation. Then, take it slow and show more openness in your face. Perhaps allow yourself to gently smile and feel this smile all throughout your body. These actions make it easier to access a soft gaze and friendly tone so you can signal comfort and safety to the others around you.

Mirror Reflection

This exercise helps you explore how facial expressions can affect your inner state. You'll look at your own face in a mirror and practice different expressions while noticing how these expressions impact your experience.

Instructions

1. Find a mirror and stand in front of it. Take a moment to get used to looking at yourself in the mirror, allowing any judgments to pass.

2. Close your eyes, completely relax your face, and when you feel ready, hold your relaxed expression steady and open your eyes. Looking at your expression, notice how it affects you. Does it draw you in? Put you off? Or make you feel neutral? People have a range of resting expressions that are normal.

3. Close your eyes again. This time, think of someone who makes you feel really good. It could be a pet or a person. Allow this thought to flow through your body, and express what you feel with your face. Now, hold the expression and open your eyes. Notice how looking at this expression affects you.

4. Close your eyes a third time. Imagine being utterly disgusted and let your face express this. Hold this expression and open your eyes. Note how looking at this expression affects you.

5. Keep your eyes open. Now, experiment with expressions until you find one that immediately makes you smile. This could be playful, warm, loving, calm, excited, or any other expression at all. Keep adjusting your expression until you make yourself break into a spontaneous smile. What would you call the expression that made you smile?

Reflection

Take some time to jot down your observations and feelings about this exercise. How did each facial expression impact your emotional state? Did any expression surprise you with the internal response it evoked?

_____

_____

_____

_____

_____

In doing this exercise, you've just explored how sensitive we can be to facial expressions, even when they are our own. Your face doesn't only show your emotions to the world; it communicates information about your nervous system: Is it in a place that is open to connection? Or is it in a defensive mode? Being mindful of your face—including shifting your facial expression to help you find your calm/connected state—will help with connection and coregulation.

Make It About the Person

Giving others the feeling of being seen deepens relationships. This is what connection is all about. And to do this, I point you back to the lesson in the previous chapter: that the core of how we can truly know ourselves is through our feelings, boundaries, and desires. This is also how we can know others.

Let's break it down. We've all had conversations that skim the surface. We discuss the weather, our weekend plans, or how our favored sports teams are doing. And sometimes these conversations stay very superficial. It's going to be a beautiful, sunny weekend. James is going wine tasting on Saturday. Edie thinks the local football team is going to do well this year. Small talk like this rarely makes people feel seen or heard. At best, these topics give us a sense that we live in the same place and with some shared activities and culture.

But buried within these topics is a path for really connecting and understanding someone better: asking questions and digging deeper so we can learn about the other person and make it about them, rather than about the topic. For example, we could ask James what he is looking forward to about wine tasting or Edie what her favorite team is in the league and why. These questions help the answerer connect with their own desires and preferences, and instantly creates a greater opportunity for them to feel seen.

The Impact of Early Messages

Sometimes, we get the message very early on that our experiences don't matter. Imagine a mother telling her young child, "You have to put on a jacket because it is cold outside." The child feels hot in the jacket, and says so. But her mom insists, "No, you have to wear the jacket because it is cold and you'll get sick if you don't." It might seem like an innocent slight, but it sends a damaging message: *Your feelings and experiences aren't important. What is more important is what the thermometer says, or what the temperature feels like to me.*

The child then might try, "It's not that cold!" or "I'll be mostly inside anyway!" If this works, then the child learns that a better way to advocate for herself—rather than sharing her lived experiences—is to argue using logic and to outsmart her mom. If Mom still insists, "Put the jacket on," and "wins," then her child learns that her experience is wholly irrelevant, and she may stop protesting and valuing her own feelings, needs, and limits.

The mom could simply be worried about her child getting ill or being uncomfortable. But coregulation and connection are very much relevant for parents relating to their children, even when there is a valid concern. If Mom's autonomic state is in one of agitation, which is highly likely, her focus will be defense (in this case, against the possibility and consequences of her daughter being wrong) rather than connection. Her daughter will automatically be hearing that shark music and is more likely to respond in kind with combativeness.

This scenario cannot promote true connection where the child feels seen and knows that her felt experience is valid. This is how so many of us learn early on to discount or dismiss our core experiences and what our bodies tell us, which in turn makes it more difficult for us to advocate for ourselves in relationships. It may contribute to why we feel safer being ourselves when we are alone, and it creates more stress when we attempt to assert ourselves with others.

A response that would result in connection and the child feeling validated would be if the mother acknowledged that her child is capable of sensing into her own desires, even if she may change her mind after spending some time outside. Being able to reflect the child's experience—"The jacket makes you feel hot, and you don't want to wear it"—would help the child understand that her reality is valid and that Mom can share in that reality. (If you are a parent yourself, see the resources section at the end of this book for educational materials on trauma- and nervous system–informed parenting.)

Seeing People at Their Core

With the same core building blocks you used to understand yourself better, you can now apply that curiosity to others. When you discuss a topic or decision with someone, assume that they have important feelings, boundaries, and desires that are worthy of your consideration. Your job is to try to learn what they are. When you shift your focus from the topics at hand to truly understanding the person behind them, you can transform your interactions.

Asking questions and being curious is great. However, if you bring in too much of your own interpretation, you make it about you, not them. "You removed your jacket. Do you not like the color?" might be too much of a stretch based on limited information. And, "You removed your jacket. Are you mad at me?" would also take the focus away from them.

Remind yourself that our minds can run off with stories, judgments, and conjectures that don't result in connection. That is why I recommend sticking with the basics to begin with: reflect feelings, boundaries, and desires. Reflecting to people who they are is an art and a skill, but sticking to the basic building blocks I've outlined here is an easy way to practice and improve.

For example, imagine you are spending the day with a friend and the two of you are deciding whether to go kayaking or visit a museum. They tell you, "I think we should go to the museum because it's supposed to rain this morning." You respond, "We could go kayaking later in the day." This is an example of what *not* to do because now the decision centers around the weather, not either of your desires or seizing an opportunity to connect with each other.

Instead, you can let the other person know that you want to see and know them by exploring their stance more. What are the feelings, boundaries, or desires they might be telling you? You could ask one or more of the following exploratory questions, all of which give the other person the chance to share more about themselves:

- Is the museum option exciting to you? (Feeling)
- Is kayaking in the rain a hard no for you? (Boundary)
- The weather aside, which would you prefer more? (Desire)

Note that these questions have an exploratory feel to them. Yes, they elicit information for making a decision, but more importantly, they give you an opportunity to connect with your friend personally. Their responses are another opportunity to let them know you value them. If they say, "I just really can't stand getting cold in the rain," you could respond with, "I get it, I want to respect your limits."

Neither of you know how you will spend the day yet, but you can start it off in a positive direction by establishing connection and safety. Doing so will put you both in the right state to find common ground and enjoy yourselves no matter what.

You can apply this lens for connection to just about any conversation, but it's especially helpful when you are getting to know someone new, there is conflict to explore, or someone needs your help to make a decision.

Suggested Questions

If you are still unsure of how to center a conversation around people rather than topics, I've compiled a list of example questions you can ask that might get you started. The questions are divided into the categories of feelings, boundaries, and desires. Consider the context of the conversation and the type of relationship you have with the other person as you decide which questions to try out with them. For example, inviting someone to share about their fears or difficult past experiences might be welcomed by a close friend but seen as intrusive by a new colleague.

Feelings
• Do you feel _____ (*feeling word*)?
• What was it like to be you today?
• Have you ever felt this way before?
• On a scale from 1 to 10, how intense are these feelings?
• Are there particular aspects that are especially challenging for you?
• Do these feelings remind you of any past experiences?
• Are you considering making any changes because of these feelings?
• Do you feel supported in processing and navigating these feelings?
• What would help you feel better or more understood?
• Are there any fears or anxieties you have about this topic?

Boundaries

- Are there specific situations or behaviors that make you feel uncomfortable or uneasy?
- How could I tell if I did something you that made you uncomfortable?
- What are the nonnegotiable boundaries you've set for yourself in personal relationships? Work relationships?
- Does something need to change so you feel safe and respected?
- How do you know when you might be overextending yourself?
- What would you feel comfortable with?
- Have you reached a limit with how much you can give?
- Are you okay with this plan? Can you let me know if you change your mind?
- Should I be aware of any signs that you're nearing your limit?
- Did you react that way because I crossed a boundary you have?

Desires

- What is your favorite part of this event?
- Are there any changes you'd like to make related to this situation?
- What activities or hobbies do you find most fulfilling and why?
- What's important to you when it comes to this topic?
- Can you describe a time when you felt truly content or satisfied? What contributed to that feeling?
- What are some things that bring you joy or make you feel energized?
- What are some of your favorite things (e.g., foods, movies, music genres)? Why do you think you're drawn to them?
- Which do you prefer?
- What "guilty pleasures" do you have? When do you indulge in them?
- What's your gut feeling about this situation?

Redirecting from Things to People

This exercise will help you practice redirecting a flow of conversation to your conversation partner's experiences so that you can help them really feel seen and deepen your relationship. I'll provide some conversation starters that center on various subjects. You may have an opinion on some of these or otherwise wish to expand further on the topic, which may make it tempting to center the conversation on the topic rather than dig for deeper connection. Your challenge will be to redirect yourself to questions and statements that center connection using the lens of feelings, boundaries, and desires.

Here are some examples to get you started:

1. Italian food is the best!

    Response: _Do you have a personal connection to Italian food?_

2. Have you read any good books lately?

    Response: _I really enjoyed a sci-fi book recently. Do you like sci-fi?_

Now fill in your own responses:

1. I wish we had a different president.

    Your response: _____

    _____

2. Social media is so bad for society!

    Your response: _____

    _____

3. My friend went to Greece last year and thought it was amazing.

    Your response: _____

    _____

4. iPhones are superior to Android phones.

   Your response: _____

   _____

5. Who is the greatest musical artist of all time?

   Your response: _____

   _____

6. What do you think we should do about global warming?

   Your response: _____

   _____

These were particularly challenging! If you struggled to redirect these conversations, you're not alone. Creating opportunities for direct connection does not always come naturally; it needs to be practiced. Know that there are no right answers, just an opportunity to practice and exercise your creativity. If you are curious, here are examples of responses that I've come up with:

1. Who would you prefer to be president and why?

2. Have you just had it with how much people are on their phones?

3. What appealed to you about what your friend told you?

4. Is there anything that would make you want to switch to Android?

5. What criteria matter the most to you?

6. Does climate change worry you? How concerned are you about it?

Yes, And

The "yes, and" principle is a rule for actors doing a scene together in improvisational theater. The idea is that when one actor makes an assertion (for example, "I can't believe the space shuttle left us behind on Mars!") the other actors will accept the reality that has been presented ("I know! It sucks") and build on the story ("Let's start working on a signal for the rescue ship"). They avoid making any negating statements ("What are you talking about? We're not even on Mars") because that would stop the scene in its tracks when the goal is to keep the momentum going. Following the "yes, and" principle encourages collaboration, openness, and adaptability.

This technique is not just for the stage; it's a practical and impactful communication tool that can help you coregulate. That's because the alternative is often adversarial. How do you feel when you offer an idea or share an observation, and someone responds in a way that is dismissive, such as "I don't know what you're talking about" or "That doesn't matter"? Does it make you feel small, like your reality isn't valid? These might seem like small slights, but they make a huge difference on the nervous system level. These dismissive or minimizing responses can send you the message that the person you are with is not someone friendly who is on your side, and therefore is someone you might need to watch out for, instigating vigilance.

I don't mean to sound dramatic or paranoid! There isn't necessarily anything nefarious going on. It's just that from a polyvagal perspective, safety and connection are anchored together, and when your nervous system senses a departure from one, so goes the other. As you continue to practice tuning in to your body's signals, you can see for yourself whether this is true.

Consider the following statements and "yes, and" responses:

1. **Person A:** I'm upset we haven't been able to spend any time together lately.

   Person B: I can understand how you would feel that way. I wish I didn't have to work so much.

2. **Person A:** You're always late to events.

    Person B: I know! It must be so annoying. How can I thank you for putting up with my tardiness?

3. **Person A:** I want us to go on more trips together.

    Person B: I loved the last trip we went on. But I don't know how I'll manage fitting another one into my budget.

It's important to note that you don't have to lose yourself and always be agreeable in order to practice "yes, and." Validating someone else's reality doesn't have to subtract from your own. Being able to make space for their reality, whether you agree with it or not, is a generous and loving thing to do for anyone you care about. From a polyvagal perspective, such altruism can benefit you as well, because the more connected others feel with you, the more anchored you are in your own calm/connected state.

Practice "Yes, And"

This exercise is designed to help you practice the "yes, and" approach in different situations, ranging from easy to more challenging. Put yourself in the following hypothetical scenarios and respond with a "yes, and" statement. Ensure your response acknowledges the other person's statement and builds upon it by adding your own constructive thoughts or questions. Practicing this will help you enhance your communication skills, encourage collaboration, and avoid adversarial interactions.

1. Your partner says: "You need to clean more."

   Your response: _____

   _____

2. A coworker proposes: "I think we should change the way we do things around here."

   Your response: _____

   _____

3. A team member tells you: "You're difficult to get a hold of."

   Your response: _____

   _____

4. Your partner says: "I think we should get a pet goat."

   Your response: _____

   _____

5. Your parent says: "You don't visit enough."

   Your response: _____

   _____

6. A mentor shares: "I'm ready to retire."

   Your response: _____

   _____

Reflection

Think of some conversations you've had where "yes, and" would have been a helpful response. How might the outcome have been different with this approach?

_____

_____

_____

_____

_____

Remember that practicing the "yes, and" principle is a journey, and it's okay to find it challenging initially. Consistent practice will help make it a natural part of your communication style, fostering more collaborative and positive interactions in various aspects of your life.

Patience and Progress

Whether the skills I presented in this chapter are brand new to you or things you already know and think about, there is always opportunity to make improvements and really fine-tune them. In some cases, the tools we use to communicate are our face and voice, and we need to consciously put effort into refining how we use them. Other tools necessitate that we shift our ways of thinking about other people and the world and tap into the power of collaboration.

Try not to be discouraged if you don't get the results you're aiming for at first. Appearing awkward or messing up is part of the learning process. It took me years before I could understand more intuitively how others read my face and voice and learn to adjust my internal state so that I could broadcast nonverbals that invite people into connection and de-escalate from hostility. Some people find this easier than others, but the skills are there for learning if you put in the work.

I've also seen that when clients are properly motivated—like when they are trying to save a relationship that is important to them—they pick up these skills quite eagerly. When the importance of seeking connection is front and center, it can be a powerful time to practice these new techniques. So, get in touch with your "why."

I want to acknowledge that employing these skills takes some emotional work. Sometimes you will have the energy for working on connection, and sometimes you won't. This is normal and okay. Whether you have the energy to put forth effort to connect—and whether that connection is sustainable—should be a consideration. The goal isn't to be constantly "on," but rather to recognize when and how to establish more profound connections so that your relationships enrich your life rather than drain your energy or cause stress.

Last, nurturing a regulated nervous system is vital for lasting well-being and can serve you in countless ways. When you mainly operate from an internal state that is calm/connected, you will be more able to use connection skills to create relationships that support you. The objective is to ensure that genuine, enriching connections become a natural extension of who you are.

This chapter was all about skills that help us invite others to step into connection with us. Next we'll explore what you need to know and do in order to make yourself available for connection and skills for facilitating it.

CHAPTER 8

Leading Yourself into Connection

Using your skills to invite others into connection is wonderful, but it's not the whole equation. Equally important is that you are truly available for the connection you are seeking. This includes proactively sharing information about yourself with others, cultivating a positive mindset about connecting, and, when you lose your ground away from a calm/connected state, being able to redirect others to help you feel safer again. This chapter will support you in exploring these skills.

While I believe the skills in this chapter will benefit everyone, this chapter may be especially relevant if you have an avoidant attachment style (to identify your attachment style, refer back to the quiz in chapter 2). People with this insecure style of attachment tend to get overwhelmed with relationships or find them to be too demanding, and they cope with this by distancing themselves. People who identify with a disorganized attachment style may at times also share some of these traits.

One reason people with an avoidant attachment style balk at relationships is because they haven't practiced the skills for stepping into connection in a way that is safe and empowering. They rightly intuit that it takes more from them than they are used to. The skills I'll introduce in the following chapter will help you create more enriching relationships by making these connections better for *you*.

To form strong bonds and connections, you'll need to feel safe with others and seen by them. This will in part be determined by the actions and behaviors of the people you have relationships with, but there are also some things that you can do to make strong and safe connections more likely. This chapter will focus on some of the skills you'll need in order to find your way toward this type of relationship. These skills will allow you, first and foremost, to prioritize feeling safe, and then to prime yourself for positive experiences.

The following skills and concepts will help you to not only express yourself, but to do so with care for your own autonomic state and that of the person you are in connection with. These skills will help you avoid the most stressful parts of—and take comfort in the safe parts of—expressing yourself.

Make It About You

The central idea of this book is that your optimal wellness hinges on your nervous system's ability to return to a calm state where connection to yourself and others is possible. Expressing yourself, the core of who you are, is an important part of feeling seen. When you say these things out loud, you acknowledge it to yourself and invite others to also acknowledge you, creating the possibility of a relationship of mutual care and connection.

The lens that is once again relevant is to share with others your feelings, boundaries, and desires. In each relationship context—from dating, to family, to friends, to work relationships—what is appropriate to share will clearly be different. But these core building blocks should guide you when considering how to share more of yourself.

First, when having a conversation with someone, what are the feelings you have about the topic, whether they be positive or negative? We sometimes balk at sharing our feelings when they are negative, but the things you have a negative reaction to are also valuable ways that people can understand you better. The times when negative emotions can cause friction in a relationship interaction is when people lash out with their feelings. This happens when feelings become overshadowed by defense states, which draw us away from the ability to connect and can make anything you say sound hostile. If you take care to stay more regulated in your experience of negative emotions, you can describe your feelings rather than lash out with them.

Next, what are your boundaries or limits in a particular situation or with a particular topic? Maybe you've reached your max for how much energy or assistance you want to offer your family member. Or someone you're newly dating wants to hang out with you on Saturday morning, but you always unwind from the week with a solo bike ride at that time. You might shy away from expressing your boundaries because you worry the other person will take it as a rejection or be disappointed with you. It might seem like the more pro-relationship move is to accommodate the other person. But this kind of thinking actually limits the connection that is possible in relationships.

By shying away from expressing your boundaries, you miss a golden opportunity to step into the relationship as an equal, someone deserving of the same considerations and understanding that you give others. Remember, a connection can't be sustainable if it doesn't include your needs as well. It's up to you to come forward and tell people what your boundaries and limits are. People who are emotionally available to connect will appreciate you for it.

Last, what do your desires tell you? By desires, I mean anything that you can connect to a longing for, like your needs, preferences, ideals, and interests. This could be as simple as sharing your favorite color and extend to how you hope a relationship will develop over time. Sharing your desires can also be new for some people. We might hide these things because we assume saying what we want will make people perceive us as difficult or will result in disappointment if we don't get what we want. So, we silently go along with decisions that don't excite us, or we try to influence decisions indirectly, without putting ourselves front and center. For example, if your friend group is trying to decide where to go for dinner, you might say, "Let's go to the sushi bar on Main because they have vegan options that Brian can eat," rather than putting yourself forward with "I'm craving sushi right now."

It might take a while to overcome the discomfort of sharing more of yourself. I'm here to tell you that the people who truly care about you want to know the real you! They want to be closer to you and understand what makes you tick.

Putting It into Words

Communicating our feelings, needs, expectations, and boundaries is very important. But we often leave these important pieces of information unsaid, simply because we didn't think to communicate it. The absence of sharing information about yourself to others can lead to miscommunication, mismatched expectations, and disconnection. In contrast, when we proactively communicate, we can avoid misunderstandings, give others the opportunity to know us better, and also practice validating ourselves.

This exercise will help you become aware of things that you could be sharing about yourself that you might otherwise not have considered. You'll select an upcoming interaction to explore your feelings, boundaries, or desires.

1. Take a moment to identify an encounter or conversation that you are anticipating with someone. This could be with a family member, partner, friend, or colleague. What was the incident? (Example: *I'm planning a dinner party for my friends.*)

   _____

2. As you anticipate this interaction, how do you feel about it? (Example: *I feel nervous because I haven't cooked for a big group in a long time.*)

   I feel _____ because _____.

3. Reflect on the boundaries or limits that you have for this particular interaction. We have limits and boundaries for every situation, even if we never approach them. (Example: *I don't want my dinner guests to stay past 10 p.m.*)

   _____

   _____

   _____

   _____

4. If the situation you're thinking of goes ideally for you, what would this look like? (Example: *I cook a delicious meal, we have interesting conversation, and by the end, we're discussing dates for the next dinner party.*)

_____

_____

_____

_____

You have just processed your feelings, boundaries, and desires that concern the interaction in question. I encourage you to share some of your insights with those you are about to share the interaction with. It could be as simple as texting, "Hey, I just want to let you know that I'm feeling nervous about cooking for everyone—but it will be a good opportunity to practice my skills in the kitchen." By sharing proactively, you make yourself more available to connect and allow others to really see you.

Positive Emotions

We often misunderstand positive emotions in relationships of all types. We imagine that if a relationship experience is positive, we should feel a wellspring of positive emotions—and that if we don't, it's because the experience wasn't that positive. Of course we want to feel these positive emotions, but sometimes, we have to put in some work to get them. To create deeper connection in our relationships, we need to intentionally cultivate positive emotions like gratitude, admiration, and celebration.

In our fast-paced world, we can quickly take people and relationships for granted. Expressing yourself when something is going well is just as important as when there is struggle. Actively noticing and sharing these moments, whether it's by writing in a journal or sharing out loud, fosters a sense of joy and celebration with those that you care about. It fuels strength and momentum in relationships, creating a nurturing atmosphere where you can flourish from feeling seen, valued, and celebrated by those who are dear to you.

I don't just mean the peak experiences that are obvious cause for celebration and appreciation, such as a wedding, new baby, or job promotion. What can be even more profound and make the biggest difference is learning to enjoy, appreciate, and find the magic in everyday moments. For instance, thanking a friend for making time in her busy schedule to have lunch or taking your call so you could hear her voice and connect. Or celebrating when your partner successfully puts up wallpaper or you are able to make dinner together on a weekday evening. This not only validates the effort that both of you put in but also strengthens your emotional connection.

At a biological level, these everyday moments of feeling safe and connected give us healthy doses of oxytocin. Oxytocin is a feel-good chemical that is released mainly when we experience closeness with others and have meaningful interactions with them. We can get big doses of it during sex or when giving birth, and we also get it in other situations where we feel safe and supported by others. Oxytocin alleviates stress and propels us toward warmth and affection. Essentially, the more you lean into these positive moments, the more you benefit from this feel-good chemical boost.

Yet it's important to acknowledge that getting close doesn't always feel good. It can be stressful, unfamiliar, or overwhelming, especially if your attachment style leans toward insecure. This can make it more difficult for you to fully immerse yourself in the joy of giving and receiving care and attention. If this is true for you, recognizing and leaning into positive moments becomes even more pivotal.

Noticing, amplifying, and sharing positive experiences and victories will help you expand into a more secure attachment style. Regularly acknowledging and sharing the good can counterbalance attachment stress and insecurity, creating a more stable and balanced relationship dynamic. For example, if you find yourself feeling stressed about the emotional distance between you and a loved one, whether it is too much distance or you feel encroached upon, reminding yourself of the things you know that they appreciate about you can reset your perspective and help you manage your feelings of overwhelm, making sure that these moments of heightened stress don't overshadow the relationship's positive aspects.

Please be mindful, however, not to use positive feelings and experiences to avoid negative ones. For example, psychotherapist John Welwood coined the term "spiritual bypassing" to describe how some people use spiritual experiences to avoid facing their unprocessed emotions (rather than as a means to explore and actually process them). There is a fine line between harnessing your capacity to focus on positive experiences and dismissing real challenges and struggles.

Instead of turning away from negative feelings and experiences, try to generate positive feelings *in spite of* and *alongside* the difficulties. For example, in the midst of a conflict with your partner, you might acknowledge that despite the difficult process of figuring things out together, you appreciate each other's perseverance and willingness to grow. Even when you have disagreements or challenges, recognizing each other's efforts and commitment can add layers of depth to the relationship.

By regularly acknowledging our positive experiences with other people, we're rewiring our brain. Focusing on these moments, paired with the emotions they elicit, reinforces their importance. Over time, you'll come to expect more good things from relationships, which in turn strengthens your ability to be resilient to stress. Noticing, amplifying, and sharing positive experiences and wins is not just about feeling good. It can be instrumental in building a solid foundation for robust, resilient, and nourishing relationships.

Evoking Positive Emotions

This exercise is designed to help you reflect on past interactions and memories that evoked positive emotions. Taking the time to recall and focus on these moments acknowledges the beauty of interpersonal relationships and the significant impact they have on our lives. For the following prompts, you can choose any relationships that matter to you.

1. The last time I felt proud of someone in my life was: _____

   _____

   _____

2. I was most recently grateful for someone's help when they: _____

   _____

   _____

3. I felt inspired by someone in my life when they: _____

   _____

   _____

4. One time I felt celebrated for who I am was when: _____

   _____

   _____

Embracing and reflecting on these moments of pride, gratitude, inspiration, and affirmation can enhance your appreciation for the individuals in your life and reinforce the positive emotions and experiences you shared together. Now that you have had a chance to reflect on these positive moments, a bonus step would be to share your reminiscing with the people who were there with you. This could be as simple as sending someone a text to say, "Remember when we . . . ? That was a great time and I'm thinking of you."

Coregulation for You

There will be moments when you are with a loved one and you find yourself dysregulated and distressed. It could be because you're struggling with bad news, you're anxious, or you've been triggered. In the past, you may have not noticed this or ignored it. Even now, you may feel compelled to continue the conversation without addressing how you feel. But as you try to carry on the conversation, you still feel off. Your body continues to ride a wave of stress.

Hopefully, you understand now that this version of you, driven by stress and survival, does not bode well for connection. You can try to "power through," but you will be fighting an uphill battle and risking more alienated connection.

You've learned a number of tools by this point to find your calm/connected home base. When you are with someone else, there are many reasons to choose the skill of coregulation—to engage in a coordinated effort to anchor a sense of safety. Because we are so vigilant to whether people are friends or foes when we are in defense mode, it's wise to recruit the other person in the effort to reset your nervous system back to home base. If you continue as is, your face, body language, and vocal tone are likely to broadcast to the other person's nervous system that something is wrong, raising their alarms and keeping the cycle going.

To coregulate, you need to deliver a dose of friendly, empathetic, or reassuring interaction to each other's nervous systems. There are no hard and fast rules about how to accomplish this. You could be more directive, if you have the capacity in the moment and know what would help you. They could take the lead if they know how to, or you both may navigate together and figure out what will work for your nervous system and theirs. With the awareness that this is important, you can redirect yourself and the other person to engage in friendly and reassuring ways to signal safety and availability of connection to your nervous system.

This is where knowing yourself well, including what makes you feel safe with other people, comes in handy. With this information, you can be empowered to take the lead and ask for what you need with statements like the following:

- Do you mind if we take a pause? I need a moment to think.

- Can I get a hug?

- Could we take a break with this topic? I'd like to just do something fun with you right now.

I often get asked, "What if I can't tolerate anything about the other person then, much less be hugged by them?" Fair question. When we are in a defense state, we often get overwhelmed with the magnitude of a problem. We doubt that the other person is on our side, and our bodies shrink away from connection because we can't access it in the moment. When we are caught in a defense state, it can be very difficult to exercise good judgment about what could be most helpful. But I'll lay out a few considerations that might help you decide what could be best for you.

First, you don't have to aim for a 180-degree change initially. If there is anything that the other person could do to make it feel even a little bit safer, you could ask for that. See if your nervous system can pick up on that shift, then build on it. Perhaps you could ask to slow down, which gives you the chance to orient yourself and remind yourself that you and the other person are on the same side. Then, perhaps, a hug would be useful.

If, however, you are too overwhelmed for any interaction to feel positive, however small, then the best course of action is to ask for some supportive space, either from the conversation topic or from the person. The purpose of this space is not to continue to repel the other person in your mind, but to help you feel supported by the space that you and the other person create for the sake of the relationship.

Limitations

Sometimes, people in our lives can't reliably collaborate with us toward a sense of safety. We may have always known this about them because we grew up with them, or we may find out through trial and error if we met them later in our life. Get to know who these people are in your life, especially if you are not willing or able to get out of a relationship with them (perhaps due to a sense of familial duty, because you work with them and can't quit your job right now, or similar). Because of their own limited capacity to coregulate, they may not share the same priority for mutual safety.

Be prepared to establish boundaries with these individuals, such as excusing yourself from tense, toxic, or negative conversations. By protecting yourself with psychological and emotional boundaries, you can limit their ability to pull you into states of dysregulation.

Save Solutions for Later

Avoid looking for solutions when you are in the heat of the moment. Instead, concentrate on finding your way back to home base, not for any other reason than your own well-being. Do not insist on solving issues—like telling your partner that they need to stop overspending—during a heated conversation. In the moment it may feel like the only way you can get comforted again is if the problem is fixed. You may even believe you are establishing necessary boundaries. But this is a fallacy. The version of you in that moment, consumed by threat, will only escalate the conflict, and it isn't capable of coming up with the best solution anyway.

You are in the best mindset to do things like asserting a boundary or coming up with solutions when you are able to do your best thinking, and that's probably *later*. When you notice your nervous system surging with stress signals and primed for hostility, your job is to ensure that your body doesn't stay marinating in this excess stress, and to use all the tools at your disposal, including coregulation, to return to your calm/connected home base. To coregulate with someone, you may need to make a request or "bid" for this collaborative practice. The following exercise will support you in making these bids for coregulation.

Bids for Coregulation

Making a bid for coregulation is about returning to autonomic home base, and nothing else. It doesn't make any promises to anyone, doesn't change your boundaries, and certainly doesn't make you forfeit anything important. It is simply the act of prioritizing autonomic safety and regulation over other things.

People can help us reorient to our calm/connected home base in numerous ways. What your nervous system needs to get there may be slightly different from what someone else needs, and what you want may also vary depending on who it is coming from. This exercise will help you sense into how you would curate coregulation for yourself by helping you identify what kind of signs and behaviors would support your nervous system to return to a calm/connected state. Being aware of the different ways that others can regulate your nervous system will help you ask for what you need next time you get triggered.

1. In the first column of the chart that follows, write the names of three people in your life you feel close to.

2. Imagine getting triggered while in the presence of each of these people. Draw lines to match each person's name to the behavior (or behaviors) that could apply. For now, ignore whether you think the other person would ever *do* the behavior. Just feel into whether the action or type of verbal reassurance would soothe *your* nervous system.

Person in My Life	Ways They Could Signal Safety to My Nervous System
_____ _____ _____	• Give me a hug or other loving touch. • Remind me of their commitment to the relationship. • Lighten the mood with a joke or change of subject. • Tell me it's going to be okay. • Tell me they see my effort. • Give me space for a pause. • Remind me of the things they like about me. • Other: _____

3. Finally, consider whether you might like to try asking your loved ones to do these things. How could you make these bids for coregulation? Planning in advance what you might say and do can help you feel more comfortable making requests in the moment, so jot down your ideas below. (For example, you might say, "I'm feeling really stressed right now. I want to continue working together to solve this problem, but first I need a break. Could we pause and hug to remind ourselves that we care about each other even though we disagree about this issue?")

_____

_____

_____

_____

_____

_____

_____

Patience and Progress

Advocating for your own needs in a relationship—taking it upon yourself to feel safe and seen—may be a new concept for you. Receiving care and feeling safe aren't always a given, especially if you have struggled with relationships in your past.

Sometimes we don't know what would make us feel safe and seen. It takes time to learn to pay attention to our body's cues and construct a sense of what makes us feel calm and connected. Before we understand this fully, it can be frustrating for ourselves and others in our lives. For instance, you may guess that you want your partner to help you think through a complex situation and ask them to do so, but when they give you the help you requested, you may not feel satisfied or seen, because practical help wasn't what you really needed in that moment.

Oftentimes the needs we have that are most elusive are the ones we have little experiencing getting. Maybe that's a hug or to be told that our sacrifice, however small, made a difference for the other person. It's important to be patient with yourself, allow space to experiment with asking for certain types of responses in conversation, and notice what seems to help move you toward your home base—and what coregulates others in the conversation—and what doesn't.

I sometimes spend an entire session with a client simply helping them get in touch with their needs in a specific situation and what would make them feel safe and seen. It is always time well spent when they finally realize the need that resonates with them deeply in their body rather than intellectualizing it.

For example, I recently met with a client who is working on expressing himself in his romantic relationship. His struggle to do so is underscored by an attachment style that runs avoidant. In this session, exasperated, he told me, "I wish my partner could just read my mind! I want her to know what's in there. But having to describe it is just so hard because I don't have the words!"

What he didn't realize yet was that his words already reflected a world of change because he *wanted* her to have access to his thoughts and feelings. Six months prior, this would have been unfathomable; both he and his partner had struggled for years with his defensive habit of keeping things from her if he thought they would upset her. Now he wanted her to know everything. In our session, we took a moment to celebrate what an incredible stride this had been for him, and to acknowledge that the hard work he had put in was clearly paying off. After the session, he felt more hopeful that continuing to put in work to communicate what he needed to his partner—and to listen to her needs as well—would continue to increase their connection.

When you put in the hard work to transform your relationships, naturally you will find moments of greater possibility for intimacy and collaboration. It's so important to celebrate these moments as much as you can. Maybe this looks like sharing with a loved one who knows you are putting the work in. Or perhaps it looks like taking yourself out to dinner. However you choose to mark the occasion, it is incredibly important to celebrate your wins on the journey toward building a stronger attachment foundation.

In the next chapter we'll explore how to stay connected and coregulate when the stakes get a bit higher—when we enter into conflict with someone.

CHAPTER 9

Staying Connected Through Conflict

Since we may all have different ideas of what conflict is, let's start with a definition. Conflict is a struggle or disagreement between people when their interests, goals, values, or opinions differ. Conflict is a natural and common part of human interactions and occurs in every setting simply because we all think and feel differently at different moments. If we address conflict in skillful ways, it can lead to positive change and resolution as well as deeper connection. But if we give in to impulsive or destructive methods or avoid talking about our differences altogether, then conflict can sow division and disconnection.

We began the introduction of this book with Marina's dilemma. She was dreading bringing up the topic of where to live next year with her partner, Alex. They have both been avoiding the conversation because their desires are in conflict, and this threatens their connection and creates doubt about whether they'll be together in the future. Marina feels ill in her stomach, has tension in her body, and ruminates about the worst-case scenarios.

You may now recognize that Marina's internal autonomic state, one that is likely in agitation or freeze, is dominating her experience of the conversation. For one reason or another, her nervous system processes this conversation as something that is a threat to connection with her partner, which is why her stress is up. Perhaps it's because Marina simply doesn't know how to have these hard conversations in a productive way. Or she's aware that this topic has already strained their bond. It could also be the influence of past trauma that activates her panic about conflict.

Marina only has so many options. Avoiding the conversation may offer temporary relief, but it only delays the conversation and plagues them both with the weight of unspoken desires and unresolved conflict. She could dive in and confront the issue in her current anxious or frozen state and hope for the best. This could be a disaster because she and Alex are already primed for disconnection, and initiating the discussion despite this could push them further apart. Instead, if Marina can find a way to ground herself, prioritize connection, and approach the conversation calmly, the dialogue could be far more productive.

Marina's situation isn't unique. Many of us grapple with similar challenges in our relationships. The essence of connection is simple: it's safety with the addition of feeling seen. Under ideal conditions, when we aren't stressed, fostering connection might feel like a breeze. Even when we are stressed, seeking support from a close confidant might be a natural fit for connection. But direct conflicts—differences in wants, needs, feelings, or opinions—pose unique challenges.

We've previously delved into various strategies to foster connection, emphasizing the importance of co-creating safety and feeling seen. All these skills and strategies are relevant for communicating in conflict. This chapter will continue to explore ways to lead with connection, especially with the unique challenges and circumstances that accompany conflict.

Leading with Connection

Many of us operate under the belief that direct conflicts inherently threaten connection. It's an assumption rooted in countless past experiences where disagreements led to distance. Yet it's essential to remember that conflict, while temporarily tense, can also serve as a testament to the depth and resilience of our relationships. It can be an opportunity not for rupture but for reinforcing the ties that connect us. It's an occasion where we can assert our commitment to making one another feel valued, understood, and respected despite our differences.

This may sound idealistic, but after many years of facilitating disagreements and conflict among couples and seeing it go every which way, I can confidently say that leading with the strength of connection is the most sensible way to address most conflict. It's a paradigm shift, but a necessary one in order to maintain close bonds. In this mindset, people in conflict convey to each other, "I'm on your side no matter what. You are safe to be yourself with me." This is the sense of belonging we all want and can appreciate.

This is especially needed when you are dealing with heightened and negative emotions. Remember, the lack of safety we feel when we have strong emotions is not caused by the emotions themselves, but by our autonomic responses to the emotions and to our surroundings, which stem from our survival instincts. This is also why others don't feel safe with us when we launch into a defense state—their nervous system responds to our shark music and begins to orchestrate its own.

You may now be thinking that defense states are the villain in this story. But remember, our defense states help to keep us alive and safe; they only become a problem if our nervous system stays stuck in these states. When our nervous system can efficiently resolve these states, it doesn't have to lead to escalated conflict. If we have the skills to coregulate each other back to safety, then these survival instincts do not hurt us and do not harm our relationships.

In the conflicts I have seen unfold that embrace and prioritize connection, people get an experience of deeper, genuine intimacy that is priceless. People shift when they experience this; most become inspired to make concessions for the relationship's sake because the relationship is such a resource for them. Additionally, because this approach also keeps them both regulated, they can think and plan without compromised cognitive skills. Any concessions they offer aren't out of desperation or urgency, but out of genuine consideration of their options and limits.

Embracing this mindset reframes the dynamic. No longer are we in search of mere compromises or ways to avoid losing something. Instead, we're after mutual understanding and acceptance. The goal becomes clear: establishing a genuine connection where both parties can feel safe, seen, and validated. When approached in this way, answers to our conflicts tend to reveal themselves, not as concessions but as pathways to deeper understanding.

If Marina and Alex were to lead with connection, they may find ways to address their needs while navigating their differences. Even if they decide to end their relationship due to their differences, they could rest assured that they have given it their best shot by not letting each other down in their handling of the conflict.

Resetting for Success and Reflection

Many of us struggle with difficult conversations that hold conflict or uncertain outcomes. If you feel this way, this would be a good opportunity to refer back to the skills you've developed for returning to a calm/connected home base.

As you might recall, when your nervous system has flagged a threat (in this case, a threat to connection), the best way to convince it otherwise is by anchoring cues of safety in the body. The simple but powerful skills you have learned to orient to safety—using a softer gaze, breathing techniques, movement, sound, touch, and so forth—are ideal to employ when you sense the challenging feelings that come up around conflict.

Instructions

1. The following list highlights some of the techniques you've learned to help yourself return to your calm/connected home base. First, draw a star next to the skills that you have found most helpful so far.

2. Next, circle the skills that aren't your current go-tos, but that you're interested in trying again or using more often in your daily life.

3. Finally, choose one skill (or perhaps more) and take some time now to practice it.

List of Techniques	
• Body Scan (p. 45)	• Physiological Sigh (p. 64)
• Diaphragmatic Breathing (p. 51)	• Hot-Air Balloon Exhale (p. 66)
• Exploratory Orienting (p. 59)	• Five-Minute Experiment (p. 68)
• Progressive Muscle Relaxation (p. 61)	• One-Hour Experiment (p. 70)

Reflection

1. As you may recall, we can use exercises like these in a call-and-response fashion to ask our nervous system to echo the calming response throughout the body. When you did these exercises just now, how did your body respond?

_____

_____

_____

_____

2. If you've found it challenging to practice these exercises regularly, what obstacles have been in your way? What steps could you take to remove these obstacles? (For example, if finding enough quiet time at home has been a challenge, perhaps you could go outside or try a short exercise during your lunch break at work.)

_____

_____

_____

_____

Pacing Yourself for Success

There are few situations that challenge our ability to stay in a calm/connected state more than being in the heat of conflict. Hearts race, palms get sweaty, and the once clear thoughts in our heads may now seem clouded by heightened emotions. Connection, in these moments, feels as though it hangs by a thread. For many, the idea of conflict being anything other than tense and disconcerting is nearly unimaginable.

Uncertainty often comes up during conflict, which can add to the discomfort. The multitude of triggers that can push our nervous systems into reactive stress and threat responses underscores the importance of slowing down. I can't stress this enough: when dealing with conflict, it's imperative to resist the natural urge to rush through it. Stress hormones, discomfort, and impatience all conspire to push us toward hasty resolutions and, in the process, escalate us further into dysregulated states.

Because there are so many things that can trip the nervous system into reactive threat or defense, your best asset is your ability to return to a calm and connected home base.

As we well know by now, when we are in agitation, fight/flight, freeze, or withdrawal, we lose our natural ability to connect. So, in the haste that we feel, we can continue to speak or explain ourselves and not notice that the other person is lost in what we are saying. Or they could have a big reaction to something we said, but we miss it because we are so fixated on getting our point across.

The only way to restore connection after getting triggered is to return to a calm/connected state. Slowing down gives you the opportunity to assess your own autonomic state while also keeping an eye out for signs that the other person may need to reset as well. Going slow allows both of you to regain your composure and reconnect.

There are many practical ways to slow down:

1. Consider breaking down the topic into multiple conversation sessions. Opt for doing less but staying regulated, rather than attempting more and spiraling out of control.

2. When speaking, adopt a slower pace—slow down your speech and stick to one topic at a time—to enable regular check-ins and to ensure that both parties are on the same page. When we're anxious or in fight-or-flight mode, we might

continue speaking without noticing that the other person is lost or has a strong reaction to our words.

3. Remember not to "crowd the plate"; exercise discipline by allowing time to process one thing before moving on to another point. Avoid introducing new topics altogether and stick with one topic at a time until you are both satisfied with it.

4. Take pauses and breathe. Resume when you are able to make eye contact in a friendly way.

5. Remember to close the communication loop. Check if the other person understands the points you are making, and whether you understand the points they are making. You can say something like, "What I hear you say is X. Is that what you are saying?" or "Do you get what I'm saying?"

6. If you notice either of you are escalating, then make a request, "Can we slow down?"

Slowing down doesn't mean avoiding challenging perspectives or feelings; on the contrary, slowing down allows you to express yourself fully while acknowledging that your words may trigger autonomic defense. Set a pace that allows both of you to process what's being said and any defensive states that emerge as a result of what is said.

The most productive conversations during difficult, tense situations are full of honesty and happen at a pace that allows people to steady themselves and each other after sudden shifts in their autonomic state. These conversations are peppered with silence, sometimes extended ones, where people remain in each other's presence, maintaining soft eye contact or even soothing physical contact as they allow each other's bodies to find a steady state.

In stark contrast, destructive conversations tend to follow a familiar, chaotic pattern. People talk over each other, introduce new topics when triggered by related issues, and lose sight of any actual goals. The overall mood escalates into a heightened sense of threat. More likely than not, no one remembers a day or two later what precisely the conversation was about because memory can become distorted when the nervous system shifts into protection and defense states.

Bringing up a Conflict

The following questions will help you identify a potentially challenging conversation and imagine how you can have it in a productive way, keeping in mind how your nervous system and that of the other person will respond to the conversation.

1. Think of a conversation you've been avoiding or dreading. Write a brief description of it. (Example: *I need to talk to my roommate about their constant late-night noise.*)

   _____

   _____

2. Identify moments in the conversation where you might feel the urge to become defensive or where the other person might become reactive. (Example: *My roommate might say, "You never told me it was a problem."*)

   _____

   _____

   _____

   _____

3. Drawing from the skills you have learned so far in this book, how could you support yourself and the other person in this conversation to feel safe and heard? List some strategies or techniques you can employ. (Example: *I can slow down, use a breathing technique, and close the communication loop by checking our understanding.*)

   _____

   _____

   _____

   _____

Remember, conversations, especially challenging ones, are a two-way street. While you can control your reactions and approach, the other person's reactions are theirs to manage. Aim for understanding, patience, and empathy, but also make sure you're setting boundaries and looking after your well-being.

Framing the Problem

Okay, so you have finally worked up the nerve to talk about a conflict, and you are approaching it with connection in mind, as an opportunity to get to know the person and to show who you are in the process. You've already gotten off to a good start. The next step is to bring the issue up with the other person.

There are a number of different ways that the problem can be framed. You can approach it in a manner that is adversarial, diplomatic, or inclusionary.

Adversarial

A classic example of the adversarial approach is "You don't appreciate me." This is where you place blame, emphasize separateness, and generally assume a you-against-me attitude. When we are in a defense state, acutely experiencing our emotions, the brain is working hard to connect the distress to the source of the problem, and we are more likely to adopt a combative attitude. During these periods of emotional hijack, the brain assigns blame to whomever is nearby. It does this not because that person is necessarily the primary cause of your strong feelings, but because they are conveniently (or inconveniently) there to point the finger at. With very little evidence or thought, our minds can spin a compelling story that positions them at the root of our distress, regardless of whether it is accurate.

Consider a scenario where someone is overwhelmed with work stress. They may come home and snap at their partner for not doing the dishes, even though their partner has had an equally exhausting day. Their brain, seeking an outlet for the pent-up frustration and seeing things with tunnel vision, conveniently pins the blame on the partner and the unwashed dishes. This explanation, even if faulty, feels satisfying because it allows the brain to justify to itself why there is a strong emotional reaction.

Diplomatic

The second possibility is to be diplomatic. A diplomatic approach avoids any direct blame but still leads with individual differences and separation. As an example, you might say, "I don't feel appreciated by you," or even "I want to feel more appreciated by you." These statements essentially describe a problem that emphasizes one's own feelings or needs and implies a bid for the other person to engage in solving it. Because they use "I statements," they may be less likely to provoke a feeling of attack.

Inclusionary

The third option is to frame the issue in a way that is inclusionary. This sounds like: "I think we've both been feeling disconnected from each other" or "It makes a big difference in our relationship when we make more time to appreciate each other." Taking an inclusionary approach brings people together by highlighting a common purpose or experience. When you do this, you have to think of the things that have already been built or established in the relationship and leverage them to guide you both in the discussion. These could be agreements that you have made with each other, shared values, circumstances or experiences that you have in common, and so forth.

The way in which you frame the problem or issue can increase the likelihood that you will get off to a positive start by setting the two of you up to be collaborators rather than opponents. Whenever possible, I recommend finding a way to frame your issue in a diplomatic manner or, ideally, in an inclusionary manner. Being diplomatic is helpful, but beginning with a common experience and making a message that brings people together is much more powerful.

For every adversarial statement, consider that an inclusionary or diplomatic framing may capture the same sentiment but better. Understanding this spectrum of ways that you can communicate allows you to be more intentional. It is very useful to know how to say things in ways that preserve the relationship rather than harm it. The following chart contains some examples of how you might approach the same issue using the three different types of statements.

Adversarial	Diplomatic	Inclusionary
You don't know how much I care about the family.	I care very much about the family.	We share the same concerns about the family.
You never let me help.	I don't want you to do it all by yourself.	We've talked about doing things like this as a team.
You never do any work around here.	I would like you to do more work around here.	We both want to live in a tidy home and need to work together to make sure that happens.
You abandoned me.	I feel abandoned by you.	We stopped being there for each other.

Each approach can have a different effect on the conversation. Adversarial framing implies that there is a winner and a loser, someone who is right and someone who is wrong. These statements will probably put the other person on the defensive. Framing the issue in a diplomatic way avoids laying blame but still emphasizes difference and sometimes division. Diplomatic statements can be useful when you already know there is a strong alliance within which to collaborate and explore differences. Inclusionary statements are built on common goals and shared values. They remind people to think of their relationship goals and promote collaboration, making this approach an excellent choice in any conflict.

Words can be incredibly powerful. Your language can guide your thinking and behavior and create openings for connection when things get difficult. You don't have to be an expert wordsmith—just pay attention to what values, agreements, or experiences you share with the other person and make an appeal to that.

Understanding and implementing inclusionary language for framing isn't about sugar-coating problems or avoiding difficult conversations. It's about ensuring that communication fosters understanding, empathy, and cooperation. When faced with issues or negative feelings, focusing on shared values and goals can help navigate the conversation toward a productive and positive resolution.

Make a habit of recognizing your autonomic state and its effect on how you communicate and bring up conflict. Practice transitioning from adversarial or even diplomatic language to more inclusionary language that underscores the collective experiences, hopes, and objectives of everyone in the conversation. This shift in communication style can help preserve relationships, create deeper understanding, and ultimately contribute to a more secure attachment style.

Practicing Communication

Your goal with this exercise is to practice framing different issues in adversarial, diplomatic, and inclusionary language. This exercise will help your brain expand the possibilities and options when communicating and giving feedback.

For each of the scenarios below, try to understand the concern or issue the person in the scenario is trying to express, including any frustration behind it. Under each scenario, you'll get an adversarial, diplomatic, and inclusionary version that expresses the sentiment, with one or more of these versions left blank for you to fill in from the character's perspective. For an adversarial version, freely assign blame and highlight what someone is doing "wrong." For a diplomatic version, avoid blame and express your feelings or needs. For an inclusionary version, focus on shared goals, concerns, or values that you can imagine in the scenario. You may need to use your imagination here and draw from your own experiences.

Here is an example with all three versions filled in to get you started:

Rami is frustrated with his partner for leaving dirty dishes all over the kitchen.

- Adversarial: <u>You always leave the kitchen in a mess!</u>
- Diplomatic: <u>I feel frustrated when the kitchen is left messy.</u>
- Inclusionary: <u>Can we work together to keep the kitchen clean? It would make our home more pleasant for both of us.</u>

Now fill in the blanks:

1. Arlene wants to spend more time with the new person she is dating, but they're not very available to spend time with her.

    - Adversarial: <u>You're too busy to find time to hang out.</u>
    - Diplomatic: <u>I want us to spend more time together.</u>
    - Inclusionary: _____

2. Jacob is upset at his mother for always appearing to favor his brother when there is a disagreement or conflict between the siblings.

   - Adversarial: _You always take his side!_

   - Diplomatic: _____

   - Inclusionary: _I think we both want to have a good relationship, and in order to do that, I think more empathy between us would help._

3. Tim is frustrated with a colleague for not doing the work that they agreed on together for a joint project.

   - Adversarial: _____

   - Diplomatic: _I'm disappointed that you didn't do your share of the work._

   - Inclusionary: _We agreed on how to split the work. What happened?_

4. Carmen is upset at Sofía for taking too long when they need to leave the house for an appointment.

   - Adversarial: _You always make us late!_

   - Diplomatic: _____

   - Inclusionary: _____

5. Lou just arrived home tired. His partner wants to talk extensively about their home remodeling project, and Lou isn't up for it.

   - Adversarial: _____

   - Diplomatic: _____

   - Inclusionary: _Let's talk about this when we both have energy for it._

Learning to use diplomatic and inclusionary language when expressing discontent and giving feedback can help you become a better communicator. There is no "right" way to express what is in your mind and heart. But understanding the effects of different options can give you new perspectives on issues and conflicts in your relationships and encourage you to be more intentional with your words.

Fielding Accusations

One of the most difficult things about conflict is the possibility that the other person, rather than address an issue in a diplomatic or inclusionary manner, will do it in an accusatory or adversarial manner. When confronted with accusatory statements, it can feel like a personal attack. There could be two primary reasons for this:

1. **Identity threat:** The accusation, if true, would call into question an important belief that you have about yourself. And this can feel deeply personal. For example, if you spend a lot of time and energy trying to please others, then someone accusing you of being selfish can be agonizing.

2. **Alienation:** If you entertain the idea that the other person believes their accusation, then you may feel deep inside that they couldn't possibly like you anymore. You may feel rejection and a form of abandonment.

The Autonomic Response

As you might be able to guess, accusations often signal threat to your nervous system, which paves the way for your internal autonomic state to shift to defense. You might react in a fight state, with your first instinct being to push back and negate what the other person is claiming: *You're wrong. That didn't happen. I don't know what you are talking about.* A dismissive response like this tends to escalate emotions and deepen the adversarial divide.

Or you may be someone who goes into freeze or withdrawal when confronted to avoid further conflict. Maybe you're quick to concede with an apology and throw yourself under the bus. This may seem like the more peacekeeping option. But your nervous system, by virtue of its activation of its defenses to protect you, is still working just as hard in the freeze state, and your body is still stressed.

Bottom line—if your body remains in defense after the initial shock of being accused, then you're more likely to react in a way that defeats connection. When you understand and can track your internal autonomic state, as you've been learning to do throughout this book, you can move toward a more constructive approach during conflicts.

Responding Constructively

The first thing you can do is navigate your nervous system back to safety. You may not be able to avoid the momentary horror that immediately follows being accused. But you can catch yourself, help your nervous system return to a calm/connected state, and then—only after you sense yourself coming back to a steady state—decide how you will engage.

What is a response that is possible if you are fully resourced? You can be open and show curiosity, no matter what the accusation is. Aim to express curiosity about what hurt the other person and why. You can do this by asking meaningful questions. Here are some good ones:

- What was the worst part of that experience for you?

- How did I hurt you?

- When did you first feel this way?

Remember, these questions must be asked without an agenda. You must not try to prove the person wrong, catch them in a contradiction, fix the issue, or gather ammunition to use in retaliation later. Try to put yourself in the other person's shoes and understand their perspective, even if their narrative challenges your sense of self momentarily.

Is this a lot to ask of you? It absolutely can be.

When people accuse you of things, it feels like a threat. But is it actually a threat? This is where discernment is useful. Just because someone says or believes something doesn't make it true. Their accusation could hold a grain of truth, or it could be an experience or story of theirs that they are projecting onto you based on hints of similarity. Just because your nervous system reactively alters your internal state to prepare for combat or shutdown doesn't mean that the threat is real. Your nervous system's job is generally to predictively overcompensate for threats, so it isn't right all the time and leads to a lot of false positives.

Although it can be a lot to ask, you are strong enough to do it. You absolutely *can* train yourself to move beyond the initial shock back into a calm/connected state. You don't have much to lose. Perhaps the worst thing that could happen is that you discover their ideas about you or their way of navigating relationships isn't compatible with yours. This can of course be painful, but it would still be useful information for deciding how close you want to be to this person.

Among couples in my office, I have heard partners make some pretty serious and terrible accusations and claims of one another. I've heard it all. I'll admit that some of these accusations even give me a momentary jolt. Partners have accused each other of everything from the illegal to the unfathomable. Most people respond automatically like they are being attacked (because their nervous systems are telling their bodies that they are), and they instinctively defend themselves by fighting back, freezing, or shutting down.

But they almost always make at least some progress toward learning to slow down and respond more constructively. I coach these partners to steady their internal autonomic state, then try to connect and be curious. When people learn to do this, they are able to create more peace in their life and their relationships.

It can be hard to hear people's opinions of you when they're negative, especially when you don't believe them to be true. But I coach people to stretch themselves because when they can open up the space for alternative narratives that are uncomfortable to hear, the relationship benefits from connection and hard-earned growth. So, I say to you again: try to stay curious. Even when an accusation feels deeply personal, approach it with genuine interest to understand the other person's perspective.

In the domain of communication, understanding and responding to accusations is like navigating a double black diamond ski slope: the pinnacle of challenges. But the practice you are putting in with the basics will eventually make even the most advanced skills easier over time and with repetition. In this case, it comes back down to tracking and shifting your internal autonomic state. Doing so resolves conflict and so much more: it fosters connection, growth, and maintaining our inner peace in less-than-comfortable situations.

Seek a Complaint

Being open to hearing complaints and accusations that people have about you without getting dysregulated is a very useful skill in relationships. Some of these complaints and accusations may hold a grain (or more) of truth, and some will be stories from the other person's experiences that they are projecting onto you. In either case, it's tremendously useful to be able to stay open and inquisitive.

Instructions

1. Choose a person who knows you well and with whom you generally feel safe.

2. Ask them to make complaint about you. If they are hesitant, then try to explain that it will help you improve your communication. Try to let them know it's safe for them to voice an honest complaint.

3. After they share their perspective, ask three questions that invite them to speak openly about what led them to experience you in this unflattering way.

4. As they respond, listen with curiosity. Your goal is to make it safe and easy for them to speak their mind without fear of judgment or retaliation.

5. After they are done, thank them for sharing their experience with you.

Reflection

1. The goal of the assignment was to get someone to tell you a complaint they have about you and be open and curious about it. How would you rate how you did?

   (Needs improvement)   1   2   3   4   5   6   7   (Fantastic job)

2. What was the hardest part of this exercise for you?

   _____

   _____

   _____

   _____

3. Think of at least one positive thing you got from doing this exercise.

_____

_____

_____

_____

Patience and Progress

Learning to address tension and conflict effectively often means unlearning old patterns and embracing new approaches. While the advice in this chapter is by no means exhaustive, it offers some useful skills for you to practice as you explore. Like with so many things, when we are equipped with effective knowledge, we can feel more confident to practice our skills.

Being mindful to slow down your pace, framing issues with more intention, and adeptly handling accusations can help you de-escalate tension and keep connection in focus. I hope you will bring what you have learned here into your real-life relationships. Practicing in the real world is how you will make progress.

Yet it's not always so straightforward as learning and practicing skills. Trauma can influence your reactions and significantly impact your ability to engage in and navigate conflict. You may notice a strong resistance to confrontation of any kind, even when it is skillful. Or, even if you understand otherwise intellectually, you might feel emotionally that expressing a negative feeling means that you have to be mean or angry, or that you will be rejected. Or perhaps when you approach a difficult conversation, you find that your brain goes to mush and you can't think well, even when you try to go slow. These reactions may stem from your brain having flagged confrontation or conflict as dangerous—in other words, trauma.

If this sounds familiar for you, know that in your journey of personal growth, it's normal to discover new underlying traumas as they come to the surface. This awareness usually happens when we reach for new goals, like the goal to stay calm in the face of conflicting perspectives.

This brings me to a final point about addressing conflict in difficult moments: it doesn't have to look perfect. Not all attempts you make will end up being as skillful as you would like them to be. A big part of making progress initially with addressing conflict is just trying new behaviors with an open and experimental attitude.

Sometimes this experimentation goes better than expected. One of my clients, Hanh, had always avoided any conflict with her mom for fear of her mom's reaction to being criticized. This had led to a pattern of Hanh's mom speaking for Hanh in situations that Hanh was uncomfortable with, like telling her what she should eat for dinner or how she should feel about a situation. Hanh wanted to start standing up to her mom instead of just ignoring it, and she worked up the courage to tell her mom in one of those moments, "That's not okay. You can't tell me how I feel. Those are my feelings." Her mother just shrugged and said, "Okay."

Another client, Derrell, told me about a time when he felt hurt by the friend and fellow artist with whom he was collaborating on a project. Derrell responded defensively by pulling out of the project in a hurry. He then discovered that what upset him was a misunderstanding after all. Realizing that he had overreacted—and may have upset a dear friend and hurt his chances for future collaborations—he felt embarrassed and regretful. But in the end, he was able to make repair with his friend by asking for grace and support after his error. His friend was happy to give it to Derrell.

Practicing conflict isn't about doing it perfectly or getting it right. Improvement will come with practice as you relax and find ways to express yourself that are authentic and in tune with your nervous system. Getting the practice in with everyday situations, forging new patterns, and proving to yourself that life is full of possibility when you do things outside your comfort zone is what really pushes you forward.

To recap, the skills you are practicing can help you be more adept at conflict, boost your confidence, and ease the chance of things escalating when addressing said conflict. But it's also useful to experiment, express yourself, allow for "mistakes," and ask for support, as Derrell did. These things aren't opposed. They can both help you rewire your brain for new possibilities and for a reality in which connection is possible through conflict. I commend you for reaching for goals that are outside of your comfort zone.

Conclusion

Welcome to the end of our journey into the connection between our internal autonomic states and the quality of our relationships. We've covered a multitude of subjects, including theories from neuroscience and psychology. My goal in presenting all this information is so that you can see what I see: that health, happiness, and safe relationships are connected and achievable.

Safety and connection—with yourself and others—are at the center of it all. Think of these as the rising tide that lifts all ships. Prioritizing these things will ensure that your experience of relationships will be less stressful. You will enjoy deeper bonds to help you navigate the stresses of life. Your mental and physical health will improve. And you will feel more fulfilled.

The trouble, though, is that safety and connection aren't always our primary experience in relationships. Whether it's because of trauma or having an insecure attachment style that suggests a less-than-optimal attachment foundation, relationships can become intertwined with stress rather than safety and connection. But the right support and effort can help you bolster your attachment foundation.

The most meaningful endeavor we can undertake in life is to equip ourselves with the knowledge and resources that nurture a nervous system that can feel safe and connected in relationships. Such a system supports our health, empowers genuine self-expression, and can offer comfort and understanding to those we interact with. If true happiness is the end goal, this should be your focus.

Practically speaking, getting in touch with our body's autonomic states and responses is how we can measure the rising tide. Learning to read your nervous system and guide it back to safety using tools for self-regulation, self-awareness, and skillful relationship communication keeps all those ships happily afloat.

Here are the key insights and practices I've gone over in this book:

1. **Identify your state:** Your journey with the nervous system starts with getting to know your internal autonomic state. For so many people, states of stress, agitation, and freeze can look and feel "fine" simply because they don't stop us from living our everyday lives. As we experience swings in how we feel internally, we have little idea to what extent we are experiencing our emotions and to what extent the physiology of survival responses is impacting our experience of feelings. Learn to recognize the signs of your body in states of calm/connected, vital stress, agitation, fight/flight, freeze, and withdrawal.

2. **Return to home base:** Everything outside of a calm/connected autonomic state requires strategic resources that take away from rest and repair. These states are meant for challenge and survival, and can't be sustained for long periods in a healthy way. The impact might be largely invisible, but the burden of long-term stress becomes more visible when we get ill. You can take a proactive role to support a healthier body by guiding your nervous system back to a calm/connected home base often. Do this through breath, movement, sound, or anything else that works for you.

3. **Address trauma:** Each individual's journey with trauma is unique and deeply personal. While this workbook touches on broad themes, it's important to continue to take inventory of how and when you get dysregulated because of trauma, especially when it gets in the way of feeling safe and expressing yourself authentically in relationships. You may need special help and guidance in this area, but it's a critical step in the healing process.

4. **Get to know your feelings, boundaries, and desires:** The beauty of knowing your internal autonomic state and promoting a more dynamically regulated nervous system is that you can better feel your feelings, sense your boundaries and limits, and be moved by your desires. This heightened awareness facilitates better decision-making and a deeper connection with yourself.

Use these three lenses to communicate in your relationships—whether it's to express who you are or to understand others better.

5. **Expand your skills for connecting:** Connection can happen in relationships of all types when people are safe in their bodies and then feel seen. The coordination of this in relationship sometimes looks seamless but actually requires a lot of skill. The skills involved include being able to do your part to effectively coregulate, express yourself, and help others express themselves. These skills make connection possible, even when there is conflict.

Change is possible. While the journey isn't finished overnight, your effort will eventually show progress.

What Progress Looks Like

Throughout the book, I've given examples of what it can look like to make progress, and it's important to remember that this isn't always obvious or linear.

You will have moments that feel like breakthroughs or goals achieved. For example, you could accomplish 30 straight days of your diaphragmatic breathing practice. This would be a milestone to celebrate. Or it will feel good when you effectively use a regulating technique to calm yourself in a moment of stress. Or you might share an intimate conversation with someone where you share more about your feelings and boundaries in a way that makes you feel closer to them. These are times when it works exactly as it should, and you should celebrate them!

But there are also times when you'll be making progress, and it won't be obvious. Maybe you'll try to attune to sensations in your body and question if you know what you're doing. Or you'll find out that an old trauma might be impacting your responses to someone, and it will be frustrating because you thought you were "over it." Or in trying a new communication technique with someone, it feels awkward and doesn't go as expected.

These moments might not feel like achievements, but they are also an integral part of growing new patterns and feeling your way forward toward more resilience and connection. And that is also worth celebrating.

Maintaining Your Progress and Continuing Growth

As you continue your journey beyond this book, remember that tuning in to your own nervous system and learning to sync with others in safety is an ongoing process, and what you have learned here is only a foundation.

Neuroplasticity and change are more powerful when you practice, reinforce, deepen, and expand your learning. Continue to immerse yourself in learning about nervous system regulation, relationships, and communication through podcasts, classes, therapy, book clubs, and support groups. Sharing with a friend what you have learned will also help reinforce your learning. The following section lists some additional resources that will support you in your continued education.

As this book draws to a close, know that I am so proud of you for the effort, insight, vulnerability, and courage that you have shown in getting this far on your journey. I wish you all the best as you keep moving toward deeper, more fulfilling connection with yourself and with those you love.

Resources

The following are additional resources I recommend, including books, social media, online courses and communities, apps, and coaching.

Connect with Me

- Extra worksheets: https://www.anniechen.net/connect
- Socials: AnnieChenLMFT (Instagram, Facebook)

Nervous System Regulation

- *Our Polyvagal World: How Safety and Trauma Change Us* by Stephen Porges
- *Heal Your Nervous System* by Dr. Linnea Passaler
- Dr. Aimie Apigian: https://www.traumahealingaccelerated.com
- Jessica Maguire: https://www.nervoussystemschool.com

Trauma- and Nervous System–Informed Parenting

- Sproutable: https://www.besproutable.com
- Circle of Security International: https://www.circleofsecurityinternational.com
- Human Improvement Project: https://www.humanimprovement.org/get-the-app
- Parent Encouragement Project: https://pepparent.org
- Jai Institute for Parenting: https://coaches.jaiinstituteforparenting.com

References

Introduction

In fact, a Harvard study spanning 80 years found that having people we can count on during tough times is what makes us most happy in life: Mineo, L. (2017, April 11). Good genes are nice, but joy is better. *Harvard Gazette.* https://news.harvard.edu/gazette/story/2017/04/over-nearly-80 -years-harvard-study-has-been-showing-how-to-live-a-healthy-and-happy-life

Neuroscientist Matthew Lieberman suggests that social connection is more basic to us than even food or shelter: Lieberman, M. D. (2015). *Social: Why our brains are wired to connect.* Oxford University Press.

Living a connected life is crucial for our social, mental, emotional, and even physical wellness: Holt-Lunstad, J. (2018). Why social relationships are important for physical health: A systems approach to understanding and modifying risk and protection. *Annual Reviews, 69,* 437–458. https:// doi.org/10.1146/annurev-psych-122216-011902

Bonding hormones like oxytocin help us combat stress, while isolation can increase our stress levels: Carter, C. S. (2022). Oxytocin and love: Myths, metaphors and mysteries. *Comprehensive Psychoneuroendocrinology, 9,* Article 100107. https://doi.org/10.1016/j.cpnec.2021.100107; Holt-Lunstad, J., Smith, T. B., Baker, M., Harris, T., & Stephenson, D. (2015). Loneliness and social isolation as risk factors for mortality: A meta-analytic review. *Perspectives on Psychological Science, 10*(2), 227–237. https://doi.org/10.1177/1745691614568352

Chapter 1

When stress is chronic, it causes a load on our bodies that makes just about every illness you can think of worse: McEwen, B. S. (2017). Neurobiological and systemic effects of chronic stress. *Chronic Stress, 1*(1). https://doi.org/10.1177/2470547017692328

Introduced by Stephen Porges in 1994, polyvagal theory looks at how our stress responses play out in a range from feeling safe to feeling that our very life is in danger: Porges, S. W. (1995). Orienting in a defensive world: Mammalian modifications of our evolutionary heritage. A polyvagal theory. *Psychophysiology, 32*(4), 301–318. https://doi.org/10.1111/j.1469-8986.1995.tb01213.x

The specifics of polyvagal theory have helped researchers understand and treat many conditions, from physical ones like chronic fatigue, fibromyalgia, and irritable bowel syndrome to mental health issues like depression, anxiety, trauma, and more: Dale, L. P., Kolacz, J., Mazmanyan, J., Leon, K. G., Johonnot, K., Bossemeyer Biernacki, N., & Porges, S. W. (2022). Childhood maltreatment influences autonomic regulation and mental health in college students. *Frontiers in Psychiatry, 13*. https://doi.org/10.3389/fpsyt.2022.841749

To do this, it can sense how safe or dangerous a situation is (what Stephen Porges calls *neuroception*) in order to decide how your body needs to respond: Porges, S. W. (2004). Neuroception: A subconscious system for detecting threats and safety. *Zero to Three, 24*(5), 19–24.

Robert Naviaux hypothesizes that the body can shut down on a cellular level by going into a "cell danger response," which complicates a lot of health problems: Naviaux, R. K. (2014). Metabolic features of the cell danger response. *Mitochondrion, 16*, 7–17. https://doi.org/10.1016/j.mito.2013.08.006

An extreme example is when stowaways have traveled in the wheel well of airplanes, and their bodies allowed them to survive the extreme conditions at 30,000 feet in the air by going into a hibernative state: Veronneau, S. J., Mohler, S. R., Pennybaker, A. L., Wilcox, B. C., & Sahiar, F. (1996). Survival at high altitudes: Wheel-well passengers. *Aviation, Space, and Environmental Medicine, 67*(8), 784–786. https://pubmed.ncbi.nlm.nih.gov/8853837

If you're curious why we would have a prosocial system, Stephen Porges hypothesizes that the prosocial system evolved 200 million years ago because it gave mammals the advantage of being able to live in groups: Porges, S. W., & Porges, S. (2023). *Our polyvagal world: How safety and trauma change us.* W. W. Norton.

You could be on your own while feeling fondness and empathy for others [in a calm/connected state]: Morton, L., Cogan, N., Kolacz, J., Calderwood, C., Nikolic, M., Bacon, T., Pathe, E., Williams, D., & Porges, S. W. (2022). A new measure of feeling safe: Developing psychometric properties of the neuroception of psychological safety scale (NPSS). *Psychological Trauma: Theory, Research, Practice, and Policy.* Advance online publication. https://doi.org/10.1037/tra0001313

This [calm/connected] is your body's true "rest and digest" mode. It's the best state for learning, thinking, and solving problems: Resnick, A. (2022, November 23). *Learning brain vs. survival brain: What's the difference?* Verywell Mind. https://www.verywellmind.com/learning-brain-vs-survival-brain-6749311

We have to talk about trauma because it is one of the obstacles that prevents our nervous system from returning fully to a calm/connected state: Dale, L. P., Carroll, L. E., Galen, G., Hayes, J. A., Webb, K. W., & Porges, S. W. (2009). Abuse history is related to autonomic regulation to mild exercise and psychological wellbeing. *Applied Psychophysiology and Biofeedback, 34*(4), 299–308. https://doi.org/10.1007/s10484-009-9111-4

Chapter 2

Psychiatrist and author Jeremy Holmes compared attachment to gravity because they are both invisible forces that keep us grounded and give us a sense of security: Holmes, J. (2014). *John Bowlby and attachment theory* (2nd ed.). Routledge.

As the founder of attachment theory, John Bowlby, famously said, "All of us, from the cradle to the grave, are happiest when life is organized as a series of excursions, long or short, from the secure base provided by our attachment figure(s)": Bowlby, J. (1988). *A secure base: Parent-child attachment and healthy human development.* Basic Books.

The original model for researching and identifying attachment styles was established by Mary Ainsworth and her "strange situation" experiment: Ainsworth, M. D. S., Blehar, M. C., Waters, E., & Wall, S. (1978). *Patterns of attachment: A psychological study of the strange situation.* Lawrence Erlbaum.

Chapter 3

This kind of awareness is sometimes called *embodiment* or *interoception*, and it allows you to understand yourself better and ultimately helps you return to your calm/connected home base more easily: Pinna, T., & Edwards, D. J. (2020). A systematic review of associations between interoception, vagal tone, and emotional regulation: Potential applications for mental health, wellbeing, psychological flexibility, and chronic conditions. *Frontiers in Psychology, 11,* Article 1792. https://doi.org/10.3389/fpsyg.2020.01792

Chapter 4

This exercise will guide you through the "physiological sigh," a calming breathing technique popularized by neuroscientist Andrew Huberman that reduces stress: Balban, M. Y., Neri, E., Kogon, M. M., Weed, L., Nouriani, B., Jo, B., Holl, G., Zeitzer, J. M., Spiegel, D., & Huberman, A. D. (2023). Brief structured respiration practices enhance mood and reduce physiological arousal. *Cell Reports Medicine, 4*(1). https://doi.org/10.1016/j.xcrm.2022.100895

For example, breathing exercises can be an amazing tool for shifting autonomic state: Zaccaro, A., Piarulli, A., Laurino, M., Garbella, E., Menicucci, D., Neri, B., & Gemignani, A. (2018). How breath-control can change your life. A systematic review on psycho-physiological correlates of slow breathing. *Frontiers in Human Neuroscience, 12,* Article 353. https://doi.org/10.3389/fnhum.2018.00353

Chapter 5

This is because when we access these fear memories, they become more pliable for a period of time through a process called *memory reconsolidation*: Alberini, C., & LeDoux, J. E. (2013). Memory reconsolidation. *Current Biology, 23*(17), R746–R750. https://www.cell.com/current-biology/pdf/S0960-9822(13)00771-9.pdf

Chapter 6

Naming feelings has been shown to be an effective way to decrease the intensity of negative feelings and it may even enhance the joy from positive ones: Torre, J. B., & Lieberman, M. D. (2018). Putting feelings into words: Affect labeling as implicit emotion regulation. *Emotion Review, 10*(2), 116–124. https://doi.org/10.1177/1754073917742706

In his book *When the Body Says No*, Dr. Gabor Maté makes the connection that his patients who develop chronic and serious illnesses are often people who suppress their internal reactions and have a difficult time saying no: Maté, G. (2011). *When the body says no: Exploring the stress-disease connection.* J. Wiley.

Part III Intro

Google's research of hundreds of teams revealed that the most innovative and collaborative teams were those where members felt safe enough to voice opinions and take risks without fear of ridicule or punishment: Duhigg, C. (2016, February 25). What Google learned from its quest to build the perfect team. *The New York Times Magazine.* https://www.nytimes.com/2016/02/28/magazine/what-google-learned-from-its-quest-to-build-the-perfect-team.html

Chapter 7

But when you are feeling unsafe or disconnected, the instrument plays ominous, disconcerting music—sometimes called "shark music," after the famously suspenseful score of the film *Jaws*—which is likely to put people on edge and make their nervous systems more vigilant: Circle of Security International. (2022, September 21). *The COS co-originators share the origins of "shark music"* [Video]. Facebook. https://www.facebook.com/100057381441315/videos/the-cos-co-originators-share-the-origins-of-shark-music-people-around-the-world-/600950278439087

Chapter 8

For example, psychotherapist John Welwood coined the term "spiritual bypassing" to describe how some people use spiritual experiences to avoid facing their unprocessed emotions (rather than as a means to explore and actually process them): Welwood, J. (2002). *Toward a psychology of awakening: Buddhism, psychotherapy, and the path of personal and spiritual transformation.* Shambhala.

Acknowledgments

I extend my deepest thanks to Stephen Porges, whose groundbreaking work has been a source of insight and inspiration for the clinical community. His contributions have profoundly shaped my understanding and approach, paving the path for this book.

My parents made certain sacrifices to give me and my brother the best life they could, and I will always acknowledge the love it took. My family, friends, and mentors continue to shape who I am and fuel me with a sense of purpose and belonging.

I am immensely grateful to a circle of friends and collaborators whose tireless support and invaluable feedback have been pivotal to this endeavor. This includes Omari Stephens, Adrien Burch, Tamara Chellam, Larry Adamson, Matt Larson, Mike Lin, Karen Montina, Forest Nelson, Vanessa Diaz, Daniel Goldman, and Melissa Kirk. Your honest critiques of my ideas have made the concepts herein clearer and more accessible.

Hundreds of clients have trusted my process to guide them, and the learnings from our sessions have helped me refine my understanding of how the nervous system actually works beyond theory.

A heartfelt thanks to Kayla Church and the entire team of editors, designers, and professionals at PESI Publishing. Their expertise, collaboration, and commitment to empowering me as an author have transformed this book from a concept into a reality.

This year of writing has been one of profound challenge and growth. It is the warmth, support, and dedication from each of you that has carried me through. I am deeply grateful for your contributions to this journey, and I share this accomplishment with all of you.

About the Author

Annie Chen is an author, therapist, consultant, and coach who holds two master's degrees in counseling and psychology. With over 17 years dedicated to studying the mind, nervous systems, and relationships, Annie has developed a unique approach to working with people. Her work integrates research from neuroscience to help clients navigate the complexities of relationships and emotional safety.

Her journey of healing through meditation, therapeutic work, and community has not only transformed her own life but also empowered her to guide others. Annie has helped thousands build fulfilling relationships and greater resilience. Her first book, *The Attachment Theory Workbook*, published in 2019, is a bestseller. She has taught at UC Berkeley, facilitated open forums, and led trainings and workshops for companies and organizations alike.

Today, Annie maintains a practice seeing individuals and couples in Berkeley, CA, and virtually. She's also a sought-after speaker, sharing her insights to inspire healthy relationships and promote a deeper understanding of the mind-body connection.

Outside of work, Annie is a mycology enthusiast who wanders near and far in search of foraging adventures.